Red Tail Captured, Red Tail Free

World War II The Global, Human, and Ethical Dimension

G. KURT PIEHLER, series editor

Red Tail Captured,
Red Tail Free

Memoirs of a Tuskegee Airman and POW

Revised Edition

Alexander Jefferson,
Lieutenant Colonel,
USAF, Ret.

with Lewis H. Carlson

FORDHAM UNIVERSITY PRESS *New York* 2017

Library of Congress Cataloging-in-Publication Data

Names: Jefferson, Alexander, 1921– author. | Carlson, Lewis H.

Title: Red Tail captured, Red Tail free : memoirs of a Tuskegee Airman and POW / Alexander Jefferson, Lieutenant Colonel, USAF, Ret., with Lewis H. Carlson.

Description: Revised edition. | New York : Fordham University Press, 2017. | Series: World War II: the global, human, and ethical dimension | Includes bibliographical references and index.

Identifiers: LCCN 2017003966 | ISBN 9780823274383 (cloth : alk. paper)

Subjects: LCSH: Jefferson, Alexander, 1921– | World War, 1939–1945—Prisoners and prisons, German. | World War, 1939–1945—Participation, African American. | United States. Army Air Forces. Fighter Group, 332nd. | World War, 1939–1945—Aerial operations, American. | World War, 1939–1945—Personal narratives, American. | Prisoners of war—United States—Biography. | Prisoners of war—Germany—Biography. | Fighter pilots—United States—Biography. | African American fighter pilots—Biography.

Classification: LCC D805.G3 J43 2017 | DDC 940.54/4973092 [B]—dc23

LC record available at https://lccn.loc.gov/2017003966

Printed in the United States of America

19 18 17   5 4 3 2 1

Revised edition

This book is dedicated to all those courageous men of color from the 332nd Fighter Group who were shot down and imprisoned in the prison camps of Nazi Germany:

Name	Prison Camp	Where and When Shot Down
Lt. Edgar Bolden	Stalag Luft I	Linz, Austria
Lt. Gene Brown	Stalag Luft I	Vienna, Austria, July 18, 1944
Lt. Harold Brown	Stalag VIIA	Linz, Austria, March 4, 1944
Lt. Alfred Carroll	Stalag Luft I	Linz, Austria, July 25, 1944
Lt. Robert Daniels, Jr.	Stalag Luft III and Stalag VIIA	Toulon, France, August 12, 1944
Lt. Clarence Driver	Stalag VIIA	Danube River, March 25, 1945
Lt. Thurston Gaines, Jr.	Stalag VIIA	Nuremberg, Germany, April 15, 1945
Lt. Robert Gaither	Stalag VIIA	Budapest, Hungary, November 22, 1944
Lt. Newman Golden	Stalag VIIA	Linz, Austria, March 20, 1945
Lt. Alfred Gorham	Stalag VIIA	Munich, Germany, February 1945
Lt. Cornelius Gould	Stalag Luft I	Hungary, December 2, 1944
Lt. William Griffin	Stalag Luft I	Rome, Italy, January 15, 1944
Lt. Lloyd C. Hathcock	Stalag Luft III and Stalag VIIA	Rome, Italy, June 1944
Lt. Lincoln Hudson	Stalag VIIA	Troppau, Czechoslovakia, March 23, 1945
Lt. George Iles	Stalag VIIA	Munich, Germany, February 25, 1944
Lt. Alexander Jefferson	Stalag Luft III and Stalag VIIA	Toulon, France, August 12, 1944
Lt. Joe A. Lewis	Stalag Luft III and Stalag VIIA	Athens, Greece, October 6, 1944
Lt. Wilbur Long	Stalag Luft III and Stalag VIIA	Blechhammer, Poland, September 13, 1944
Lt. Richard Macon	Stalag Luft III and Stalag VIIA	Montpellier, France, August 12, 1944
Lt. Walter McCreary	Stalag Luft III and Stalag VIIA	Kaposvár, Hungary, October 22, 1944
Capt. Armour McDaniel	Stalag VIIA	Berlin, Germany, March 31, 1945
Lt. Woodrow Morgan	Stalag Luft III and Stalag VIIA	Rome, Italy, May 26, 1944
Lt. Starling Penn	Stalag Luft I	Linz, Austria, July 25, 1944
Capt. Lewis C. Smith	Stalag Luft III and Stalag VIIA	Florence, Italy, June 6, 1944
Lt. Luther Smith	Hospital and Stalag 17A	Spittal, Austria, October 13, 1944
Lt. Floyd Thompson	Stalag Luft III and Stalag VIIA	Forli, Italy, June 29, 1944
Lt. Quitman Walker		Hungary, November 22, 1944

Lt. Charles Williams	Stalag Luft III and Stalag VIIA	Yugoslavia, July 30, 1944
Lt. Kenneth Williams	Stalag Luft III and Stalag VIIA	Athens, Greece, October 4, 1944
Lt. Henry Wise	Stalag Luft I	Ploiesti, Romania, August 26, 1944
Lt. Carrol S. Woods	Stalag Luft III and Stalag VIIA	Athens, Greece, October 6, 1944

Contents

Foreword

Lewis H. Carlson

I first met Alexander Jefferson in 1993 when I interviewed him for a book on World War II prisoners of war.[1] He was one of 32 Tuskegee Airmen from the 332nd Fighter Group who was shot down defending a country that still considered blacks to be second-class citizens. He, like thousands of other African Americans, including 992 Tuskegee Airmen, had fought against Hitler's racism in a military so segregated that even its blood plasma was separated by race.

I met him again several years later when he was an honored guest at the Celebrate Freedom Festival in Pigeon Forge, Tennessee. Jefferson, who had retired as a lieutenant colonel from the U.S. Air Force Reserve on July 1, 1969, happened to be the ranking officer among the several former prisoners of war being honored that day, but he was the only African American. I thought to myself, "What a fascinating slice of history!" Here is a man who as a young black student in Atlanta, Georgia, lived in such a racially proscribed world that he was not even allowed to walk in the city's parks. Now he is giving an inspirational address to an appreciative, overwhelmingly white audience in one of the former states of the Confederacy.

When Alexander Jefferson was commissioned a second lieutenant in the U.S. Army Air Corps in 1944, white America thought it knew its African Americans. Unfortunately, what it knew came largely from cultural stereotypes that were meant to reassure insecure whites that blacks needed to be kept firmly in their place. Black women were seen as fat, jovial Aunt Jemimas who nurtured appreciative white youngsters. Black men, on the other hand, were expected to play the "coon," afraid of their own shadow, and always clowning for the amusement of white audiences. A movie actor named Stepin Fetchit became a star in the 1930s and early 1940s playing a shuffling, lazy, chicken-stealing child-man. These same stereotypes could also be found in popular songs, novels and short stories, crude cartoons, and on weekly radio shows. In short, here was something less than a man who clearly was not ready for full citizenship, let alone capable of flying an airplane. That such images did not

I was treated better as a POW than I was back home.
—Lt. Colonel Alexander Jefferson

reflect reality mattered little to the majority of white Americans, for whom a genuine African American—say, a Tuskegee Airman—became, in the unforgettable words of novelist Ralph Ellison, "an invisible man."

It was not only the creators of popular culture who distorted or denied the existence of millions of African Americans. Scholars and intellectuals were equally guilty. After the Civil War, white historians made it painfully clear that blacks were ill-equipped to handle their newfound freedom—and to prove their point, they portrayed the Reconstruction era as a time of misrule by carpetbaggers, scallywags, and ignorant blacks. Such an interpretation, of course, ignored the fact that many of the antebellum free blacks who returned to represent the South in state and national legislatures had been well educated, either in northern colleges or abroad, and even some of the former slaves had at least as much formal education as the old Illinois rail-splitter who became president of the United States.

Clearly, in the post–Civil War decades, it was not blacks who were unable to handle their newfound freedom, but rather whites, who now projected their own moral and societal shortcomings onto the object of their aversion. The result was the enforcement of a rigidly segregated society—overtly in the South, covertly in the North—that sought to control and confine the unwanted and unacceptable phenomenon of free and equal blacks.

As a further rationale for this Jim Crow America, whites also created a nostalgic view of slavery in which happy and contented blacks were clearly better off than their emancipated brethren who seemed incapable of surviving as free Americans. Joel Chandler Harris' invention of the wise and kindly Uncle Remus was typical, as were the many maudlin songs of Stephen Foster and, several decades later, the unforgettable plantation images of Margaret Mitchell's *Gone with the Wind* and its many imitators. This "3-M" interpretation of slavery—with all its moonlight, magnolia blossoms, and sticky molasses—also found acceptance among many white historians, and not all of them Southerners. Slavery, concluded U. B. Phillips (a prominent Georgia-born white historian who taught at the Universities of Michigan, Wisconsin, and Yale in the early twentieth century), although not necessarily an admirable institution, was nevertheless the "best school" for developing "a fairly efficient body of laborers out of a horde of savages." As late as the 1950 edition of their textbook *The Growth of the American Republic*, Henry Steele Commager and Samuel Eliot Morison, two of

America's most distinguished and widely read liberal, Northern historians, wrote, "As for Sambo, whose wrongs moved the abolitionists to wrath and tears, there is some reason to believe that he suffered less than any other class in the South from its 'peculiar institution.'"[2]

Similarly, prominent scientists in the early twentieth century were equally convinced that blacks were permanently trapped on the lower rungs of the evolutionary ladder. To prove the point, in 1906, the New York Zoological Society placed an African pygmy by the name of Ota Benga and an orangutan together in a cage. In 1927, Yale geographer Ellsworth Huntington wrote, "[Negroes] and their slavery have been enemies to the children of the Builders," while in the same year Harvard geneticist Edward Murray East concluded, "Mentally the African negro [sic] is childlike, normally affable and cheerful, but subject to fits of fierce passion. . . . We can find no probability that the negro will contribute hereditary factors of value to the white race." And for the University of Virginia's Robert Bennett Bean, writing in 1935, "The size of the brain in the Black Race is below the medium both of the Whites and of the Yellow-Browns."[3]

That such pseudoscience and deformed history reflected preconceived notions of racial superiority rather than scholarly research or empirical evidence seems obvious today, but often overlooked is how such distorted thinking adversely affected African Americans' historic struggle for civil rights and professional opportunities, regardless of their individual and collective accomplishments. The history of African American participation in military service is a case in point.

In spite of the resistance of military and political leaders, African Americans have willingly, and often heroically, fought and died in every American military conflict, going as far back as the eighteenth-century skirmishes and wars against the Indians, French, and, of course, the British. Unfortunately, 250 years of military duty and sacrifice have all too often been ignored, or else trivialized by allowing a heroic name or two to creep into the record. Crispus Attucks, who died in the 1770 Boston Massacre, comes immediately to mind, but playing a much greater role in the colonial struggle for independence were the 5,000 free and enslaved blacks who fought in the Continental Army, various state militias, and the budding American navy. To be sure, fighting for a fledgling government that sanctioned slavery was a difficult decision, and there were those African Americans who joined the British loyalists in return for the promise of freedom. Indeed, it was such promises by the British that forced George Washington and his generals to reverse their earlier policy of opposing the enlistment of blacks.

The contributions of African American soldiers and sailors in the Revolutionary War helped fuel the abolitionist movement in the North, leading to the end of slavery in several Northern states, but they did not result in equal opportunities in the military. After the war, the army restricted itself to a small number of black scouts and guides; and in 1798, the newly formed U.S. Marine Corps totally excluded "Negroes, mulattos, and Indians."

Initially, the navy afforded African Americans more and better opportunities than did the army, largely because of a shortage of willing white recruits and also because many white sailors, appalled by the living conditions aboard the ships, deserted. Blacks fought in the First Barbary War of 1801–1805 and in the War of 1812, where approximately 10 percent of the sailors were black. Of the 50 black seamen who fought with him at the Battle of Lake Erie, Captain Oliver H. Perry said, "They seemed absolutely insensible to danger."[4] In the Civil War, one in every four of the 118,000 Union sailors was black, and at least four were awarded the Medal of Honor.[5] In spite of such promising beginnings, the subsequent status of African Americans in the U.S. Navy steadily declined until by World Wars I and II, they were allowed to serve only as stewards or messmen. The navy's top brass explained this decision by insisting that blacks lacked the mental and technical abilities to master the technology of the modern navy.

Relatively few black soldiers participated in the land battles of the War of 1812, but General Andrew Jackson promised those who fought with him in the Battle of New Orleans that "the American nation shall applaud your valor, as your general now praises your ardor."[6] Unfortunately, such was not the case, and an 1820 U.S. Army order prohibited any further recruitment of blacks.

The Civil War provided an enormous opportunity for African American soldiers again to prove their mettle. Inspired by Frederick Douglass, who promised that "slaves and free colored people [would form] a liberating army, to march into the South and raise the banner of emancipation among the slaves,"[7] thousands of African Americans eagerly sought to enlist. Initially, Lincoln refused to use black troops, fearing they would prove inadequate and that "half the Army would lay down their arms and three other states would join the rebellion."[8] Despite Lincoln's reticence, many slaves abruptly fled their masters and joined the invading Northern forces, usually serving in support roles or as sentries. Finally, after flagging enlistments, mounting casualties, and increasing pressure from abolitionists forced the president's hand, Lincoln agreed in 1862 to the enlistment of African Americans.

More than 183,000 African Americans served in the Union army. Called the United States Colored Troops (USCT), 93,000 of them came from the slave states, thereby contradicting those white Southerners who insisted that their slaves were content with the "Peculiar Institution." Another 40,000 came from the border states, and the remaining 53,000 from the free states. After 1862, blacks fought in every major campaign, serving in the infantry, cavalry, and artillery and as engineers and scouts. More than 38,000 lost their lives, a mortality rate nearly 40 percent higher than that suffered by their white counterparts.

Most celebrated was the 54th Massachusetts Volunteer Infantry Regiment, whose march into Charleston, South Carolina, was immortalized 124 years later, not in traditional history books but in Edward Zwick's 1989 movie *Glory*. Other black units also made significant contributions to the Union cause, but such wartime heroics did not translate into peacetime opportunities, and the only black units to remain on active duty after the cessation of hostilities were the 24th and 25th Infantry Regiments and the 9th and 10th Cavalry Regiments, later known as the Buffalo Soldiers for their exploits on the frontier fighting Indians.

The Buffalo Soldiers also played a prominent role in the Spanish-American War; in fact, the 10th Cavalry, under Captain John J. Pershing, known as "Black Jack" for his leadership of African American troops, may well have reached the top of San Juan Hill before Colonel Theodore Roosevelt's renowned Rough Riders. Indeed, they fought so well that one Southern-born white officer later admitted, "If it had not been for the Negro cavalry the Rough Riders would have been exterminated."[9]

Black soldiers also fought against the Philippine insurgents between 1899 and 1902, but in spite of their recurring military accomplishments, their treatment had not noticeably improved by 1917, when the United States entered World War I to make the world safe for democracy.

Although still barred from the Marines and not allowed in the Army's Aviation

Corps, more than 367,000 African Americans served in World War I. All served in segregated units, except for those fortunate enough to fight with the French.

The first black soldiers to land in Europe worked primarily as laborers and stevedores. The first combat unit was the 369th Infantry Regiment, assigned to the French, who welcomed them as fellow soldiers rather than as porters needed to carry or clean equipment. From April, 1918 until the end of the war—191 straight days on the front lines—the 369th conducted itself as admirably as any American unit in Europe. They were the first Allied troops to reach the Rhine, and they never lost a man to capture or ever retreated in the face of German attacks. The Germans called them "Hell Fighters," and the French awarded the entire regiment the Croix de Guerre and honored 171 of its individual soldiers with either the Croix de Guerre or the Legion of Honor.

The 370th, 371st, and 372nd Infantry Regiments were also assigned to the French "Red Hand" Division. Along with the 369th, their accomplishments were such that French General Mariano Goybet proudly proclaimed, "These crack regiments overcame every obstacle with a most complete contempt for danger. . . . Through their steady devotion, the 'Red Hand Division' . . . was constantly leading the way for the victorious advance of the Fourth Army."[10]

Unfortunately, once again, wartime achievements did not result in improved conditions for blacks, either in the military or on the home front. In August 1918, a document titled *Secret Information Concerning Black Troops* warned the French that intermingling with black troops would lead to the assault and rape of white women. That the French ignored such advice simply made white Americans more determined than ever to reassert their control over the lives and destinies of African Americans after the country returned to normalcy.

The returning Expeditionary troops were enthusiastically welcomed by huge parades in many northern cities, and scattered among them were several black units, but their moment of glory was short-lived. Triggered by the Red Scare, a resurgent nativism, a revitalized Ku Klux Klan, and a lack of leadership in Washington, these postwar years were among the most racially violent in American history. President Woodrow Wilson, who even before the war had issued an executive order segregating all government offices, restaurants, and restrooms, as well as effectively eliminating blacks from the civil service, was certainly not going to encourage domestic civil and economic rights after the armistice. More than 100 blacks were lynched in 1919 and

1920, including many former soldiers, some of whom were still proudly wearing their uniforms. Over the next few years, deadly race riots broke out in both northern and southern cities, the worst of which occurred in Chicago in July, 1919, when 15 whites and 23 blacks lost their lives, and two years later in Tulsa, when 21 blacks and nine whites were killed. The racial climate had scarcely improved, when, on October 30, 1925, the War Department distributed a memo titled *The Use of Negro Man Power in War*. Totally ignoring African Americans long and often illustrious record in combat, the War Department argued that the black soldier be restricted to maintenance units because he "was physically unqualified for combat duty [and was] by nature subservient, mentally inferior, and believed himself to be inferior to the white man." In addition, he was "susceptible to the influence of crowd psychology, could not control himself in the face of danger, and did not have the initiative and resourcefulness of the white man."[11]

In September, 1940, in preparation for an even more deadly and destructive world war, Congress enacted the Selective Training and Service Act. Reacting to increasing African American demands for a more equitable role in the military, this first peacetime draft called for blacks to be trained for combat but only in segregated units. The U.S. Army Air Corps, which in World War I had rejected all African American applicants because "it was impossible to mix blacks with whites,"[12] now grudgingly admitted blacks, although also only in segregated units. A War Department memo sent to President Roosevelt on October 8, 1940, rationalized this decision, arguing that experimenting with integrated units "would produce situations destructive to morale and detrimental to the preparations for national defense."[13] From these contrary but fateful decisions emerged the Tuskegee experiment to train black pilots.

More than three million African Americans registered for the draft, and approximately one million served on active duty, but the questions persisted: Would their fighting abilities be fully utilized, and would their military achievements translate into a more open society for all blacks in postwar America? Looking back after the passage of more than one-half century, one has to conclude that the government's response was more positive and proactive than it ever had been in the past.

President Harry S. Truman took the first steps. The 1947 report of his Civil Rights Commission, *To Secure These Rights*, concluded, "The war experiences brought to our attention a laboratory in which we may prove that the majority and minorities of our population can train and work and fight side by side in cooperation and harmony."[14] The next year, Truman issued Executive Order 9981, mandating the integration of the armed forces. Clearly, the achievements of the Tuskegee Airmen and other black combatants played a pivotal role in the president's decision, as they did in advancing the civil rights movement of the 1950s, but the struggle was never smooth or easy. The U.S. Army and the Marines still went into battle in the Korean War in segregated units, although battlefield necessities often forced the intermixing of white and black troops. Not until September, 1954 was the secretary of defense able to announce that the last all-black unit had been abolished. Another important step was taken in July, 1963 when Secretary of Defense Robert McNamara ordered the elimination of off-base discrimination. Thereafter, the armed services' record in affording African Americans fair and equal career opportunities has matched or exceeded anything found in the civilian sector.

For years after the end of World War II, the majority of Americans, including many African Americans, had no idea that black fighter pilots fought in World War II, let alone that they had such a sterling record of achievement. And even after learning of the heroic exploits of the Tuskegee Airmen, it was difficult for most white Americans to put aside the pervasive stereotypes that had clouded their judgment. Where, they wondered, had the Air Corps found men of this caliber? Surely not from among all those eye-rolling, shuffling Amos-and-Andy characters with which they were so familiar. Simply put, most white Americans had never seen, let alone met, a black physician, educator, lawyer, or pilot.

There were, of course, as Alexander Jefferson's story makes clear, thousands of African American families with academic and professional pedigrees just as impressive as those found in the white community. In fact, the average Tuskegee Airman had better academic credentials than his white counterpart. Jefferson, who came from a long line of prominent clergymen and educators, was typical. He had completed undergraduate majors in biology and chemistry and had taken graduate courses in chemistry. In addition, he had worked as a chemist before joining the Tuskegee program and also exhibited considerable artistic talents.

As exceptional as many of the African American pilots were, their struggle for acceptance was never easy. West Point graduate Benjamin O. Davis, Jr., who was in the first graduating class of Tuskegee Airmen in 1942, well understood the challenges of surviving and overcoming the racist individuals and institutions that wanted him to fail. As had been the case with earlier blacks who had attended the U.S. Military Academy, his fellow cadets not only refused to room with him but also gave him the "silent treatment," never speaking to him during his four years of study. However, such affronts only made this future lieutenant general more determined. He wrote, "All the blacks in the segregated forces operated like they had to prove they could fly an airplane when everyone believed they were too stupid. [But] we would go through any ordeal that came our way, be it in garrison existence or combat, to prove our worth."[15]

Archie Williams was one of the few black instructors at the Tuskegee Army Airfield. He possessed three university degrees, including one in engineering from the University of California, Berkeley, and an Olympic gold medal, won in the 400-meter dash at the 1936 Berlin Olympics. Williams knew that white America expected his students to fail, but he also knew that this would not be the case. With tongue-in-cheek drollery, he noted, "After all, we were the cream of the crop."

> We knew the whites in charge figured, "We'll get these niggers in a bunch of airplanes and let them kill themselves, and that will be that." But the funny part of it was that they skimmed the cream of the crop out of the colleges. We had guys with PhDs, physicians, engineers—two of them even became four-star generals. These guys were hand-picked, so there was no way we were going to flop.[16]

Archie Williams was right. The 450 Tuskegee-trained fighter pilots of the 99th Fighter Squadron and the 332nd Fighter Group flew more than 15,000 sorties and 1,500 missions over North Africa and Europe. During their more than 200 missions, which involved escorting bombers to and from their targets, the "Red Tail Angels"—as the custom-painted P-51 Mustangs of the 332nd were affectionately called by the bomber crews they were protecting—never lost a single bomber to enemy aircraft. They were also credited with damaging or destroying 409 German aircraft and even one destroyer. Sixty-six of these brave men were killed in combat, and another 32, including Alexander Jefferson, were shot down and became prisoners of war.

Even after proving themselves in combat against the Luftwaffe, Jefferson and his fellow Tuskegee Airmen returned to a country that continued to treat them as second-class citizens. Consider the humiliation, as Jefferson describes it, of coming down the gangplank in the shadow of the Statue of Liberty and being ordered by a young, white private, "Whites to the right, niggers to the left."

Of course, American society would eventually change, and the armed forces have certainly been in the vanguard in offering increasingly attractive career opportunities for African Americans. Much slower has been the civilian sector, but here too social and economic possibilities gradually improved, at least for the black middle class and the former Tuskegee Airmen.

In retrospect, the Tuskegee Airmen were indeed heroic warriors—the Germans called them *Schwarze Vogelmenschen*, or Black Birdmen—but their achievements were not limited to the battlefields of World War II. After returning home, some became very successful in the civilian sector. Others stayed in the military and played important roles in integrating the armed forces, including two who became four-star generals, and one who earned three stars. Without exception, all continued their struggle for civil rights, and not just for African Americans, as Alexander Jefferson once explained, "but for all humankind in the United States."

Notes

1. Lewis H. Carlson, *We Were Each Other's Prisoners: An Oral History of World War II American and German Prisoners of War* (New York: Basic Books, 1997).

2. Lewis H. Carlson and George A. Colburn, *In Their Place: White America Defines Her Minorities, 1850–1950* (New York: John Wiley & Sons, 1972), 107–08.

3. Ibid., 99–106.

4. John Hope Franklin, *From Slavery to Freedom: A History of Negro Americans* (New York: Knopf, 1947, 1997), 124.

5. Lerone Bennett, Jr., *Before the Mayflower: A History of Black America, 1619–1962*, 4th ed. (Chicago: Johnson, 1969), 394.

6. Ibid., 125.

7. David Herbert Donald, *Lincoln* (New York: Simon & Schuster, 1995), 367.

8. Ibid.

9. Franklin, *From Slavery to Freedom*, 310.

10. Ibid., 345.

11. "The Use of Negro Man Power in War," 30 October 1925, Albert F. Simpson Historical Research Center, MAFB; quoted in Alan Osur, *Blacks in the Army Air Forces During World War II: The Problem of Race Relations* (Washington, DC: U.S. Government Printing Office, 1977), 2.

12. William Alexander Percy, "Jim Crow and Uncle Sam: The Tuskegee Flying Units and the U.S. Army Air Forces in Europe During World War II," *The Journal of Military History 67* (July 2003), 775.

13. Ibid., 776.

14. Ibid., 810.

15. Quoted in General Benjamin O. Davis, Jr. obituary, *The New York Times*, July 7, 2002.

16. Personal interview. See also Lewis H. Carlson and John J. Fogarty, *Tales of Gold: An Oral History of the Summer Olympic Games Told by America's Gold Medal Winners* (Chicago: Contemporary Books, 1987), 144–58.

Preface to the Revised Edition

Even before the United States officially declared war after Japan's surprise attack on Pearl Harbor on December 7, 1941, the U.S. War Department began setting up an "experimental," albeit segregated base, as were all American units at the time, to train black pilots. Headquartered at Tuskegee, Alabama, in the heart of the Old Confederacy, the camp officially opened on July 23, 1941. By war's end, 992 African American pilots had graduated and fought for their country against the Axis Powers. In 1947, this so-called experiment ended, and Tuskegee closed its doors. Nevertheless, President Harry S. Truman ordered an end to military segregation, which also contributed to a totally independent Air Force, Army, and Navy.

Future General Benjamin O. Davis, Jr., who had been among the initial African American graduates of West Point, became cadre and then commander of the 99th Fighter Squadron, which was the first of the units to be formed by Tuskegee graduates. The 99th, and later the 332nd Fighter Squadron, earned an exemplary combat record, flying 1,578 missions, damaging or destroying 410 enemy aircraft, and flying more than 200 escort missions protecting the bombers in their care.

Individual honors among the Tuskegee graduates included 744 Air Medals, 95 Distinguished Flying Crosses, 14 Bronze Stars, 8 Purple Hearts, a Legion of Merit, and a Silver Star. Collectively, the Tuskegee Airmen earned a Presidential Distinguished Unit Citation for exceptionally meritorious service that contributed materially to the winning of the war, from which 66 Tuskegee Airmen never returned.

Following in the footsteps of the 99th and 332nd groups, the 477th Bombardment Group also trained at Tuskegee, but the war ended before its members saw action.

From the ranks of the Tuskegee Airmen came many distinguished Americans, including the Honorable Coleman A. Young, who served a record five terms as Mayor of Detroit. Three became Air Force generals, one became a state lieutenant governor, and others served as members of Congress, physicians, lawyers, and in various other prominent positions in their respective communities.

In July, 1972, in Lt. Colonel Alexander Jefferson's basement, several of these heroic men formed the Tuskegee Veterans Association. Their goal was not only to rekindle the memories and friendships that had been forged in the hot blast of war's furnace but to establish an organization that could spread their good works nationally. As of this writing, the 37 chapters of the Tuskegee Airman publish books, fund education, support scientific and social research, and extend scholarships to those in need. All grants are made in accord with Dr. Martin Luther King, Jr.'s vision of a color-blind society in which no consideration is given to race, creed, or color. Their Distinguished African American Award is given annually to that individual deemed to have best served America with honor, equality, and patriotism.

Alexander Jefferson Timeline

November 15, 1921	Alexander Jefferson born in Detroit, Michigan
June 1938	Graduates from Chadsey High School in Detroit, Michigan
September 1938	Begins his college studies at Clark College in Atlanta, Georgia
June 1942	Graduates from Clark College with majors in chemistry and biology and minors in mathematics and physics, and returns to Detroit, Michigan
September 23, 1942	Sworn in to the U.S. Army Reserves
September 1942	Begins graduate school at Howard University in Washington, DC
April 13, 1943	Called to active duty to begin flight training
May 2–July 1, 1943	Pre-flight training at Tuskegee Army Airfield, Alabama
July 2–September 1, 1943	Primary flight training at Tuskegee Institute
September 2–November 1, 1943	Basic flight training at Tuskegee Army Airfield
November 2, 1943–January 6, 1944	Advanced flight training at Tuskegee Army Airfield
January 7, 1944	Graduates and receives his wings as a second lieutenant in the U.S. Army Air Corps
January 7–February 5, 1944	1155th SE: P-40 training at Tuskegee Army Airfield
February 5–May 10, 1944	553rd Replacement Squadron:Training in P-39s at Selfridge Army Air Base, Detroit, Michigan
May 12–26, 1944	Training in P-39s at Walterboro Army Airfield, South Carolina
May 27–June 8, 1944	En route to overseas assignment
June 8–13, 1944	Oran, Algeria
June 15–19, 1944	Naples, Italy
June 20–August 12, 1944	Ramitelli Air Base in southern Italy, combat replacement pilot in the all-black 332nd Fighter Group
August 12, 1944	Shot down over southern France and becomes a POW

August 18–20, 1944	POW in Oberursel, Germany, near Frankfurt
August 20–23, 1944	Interned in Dulag Luft, Wetzlar, Germany, for interrogation
August 26, 1944	Arrives in Stalag Luft III at Sagan, Germany
January 27, 1945	Evacuates Stalag Luft III
February 3, 1945	Arrives in Stalag VIIA at Moosburg, Germany
April 29, 1945	Liberation!!
June 5–10, 1945	Fort Dix
June 7, 1945	Arrives home in New York
June 7–August 18, 1945	Leave, processing, and reassignment, Atlantic City, New Jersey
June 10–August 1945	60-day recuperation
August 10–18, 1945	Atlantic City
August 15, 1945– January 1, 1946	Instrument and flying instructor, Tuskegee Army Airfield
August 18–25, 1946	TAAF; 2143RD AAFBU Sq
August 25, 1946	Instrument SE Instr A.C. TAAF
August 26, 1946	318th AAFBU Lockbourne AAB Columbus, Ohio
October 16, 1946	Marries Adella Tucker McDonald
January 16, 1947	Discharged from active duty but joins the Air Force Reserve
September 1947– June, 1948	Takes science education classes and earns a teaching certificate at Wayne State University, Detroit, Michigan
September 1948	Begins teaching science at Duffield Elementary School, Detroit, Michigan
June 7, 1949	Birth of daughter Alexis
August 21, 1951	10th AF (VRS)(CONAC)(Res)
April 1, 1953	9607th ARes Sq (CONAC) Lonyo 9126th ARES GP
June 1954	Receives MA in education from Wayne State University
September 1954	Moves to Pattengill Elementary School, Detroit, Michigan
August 12, 1956	16-Day Air Command & Staff
January 14, 1957	Gen Trng Flt 'A' 9504th Air Res Sq
August 1, 1958	AFSC 7535: 3504th Sq Staff Admin Off
August 5, 1958	AFSC 7535. Instructor 2653nd ARC (CONAC)
April 19, 1959	AFSC 7324 Personnel Officer Course
June 1, 1960	Completes 30 hours of graduate work in education beyond his MA

July 1, 1960	AFSC 7376 9612th AR Sq Selfridge AFB
July 1, 1961	AFSC 7516 Educ & Trg Staff Off 9504th AFRR Sq Willow Run Arpt (CONAC)
July 1, 1969	Retires from the Air Force Reserve as a lieutenant colonel
September 9, 1969	Appointed Assistant Principal of Hally Elementary School, Detroit, Michigan
September 1970	Appointed Assistant Principal of Ferry Elementary School, Detroit, Michigan
July 12, 1972	One of the organizers of the Detroit Chapter of the Tuskegee Airmen, the first chapter
July 1974–July 1996	Serves as president of the Detroit Chapter of the Tuskegee Airmen
1978–present	Serves as a voluntary admissions counselor for the U.S. Air Force Academy
June 1979	Retires from the Detroit Public Schools
October 14, 1995	Enshrined in the Michigan Aviation Hall of Fame at the Kalamazoo Air Museum, Kalamazoo, Michigan
June 1996	Rouge Park Radio Controlled Model Airplane Club (Detroit) is renamed the Alexander Jefferson Flying Field
1998	Received honorary Doctorate of Humanities degree from Tuskegee University
April 29, 2007	Tuskegee Airmen awarded the Congressional Gold Medal
May 2016	Awarded the Bronze Star
November 12, 2016	Presented the French Knight of the Legion of Honor Medal

Red Tail Captured, Red Tail Free

Alexander Jefferson built this model P-51 Mustang Red Tail, which is a reproduction of the actual plane he piloted in combat during World War II.

Introduction

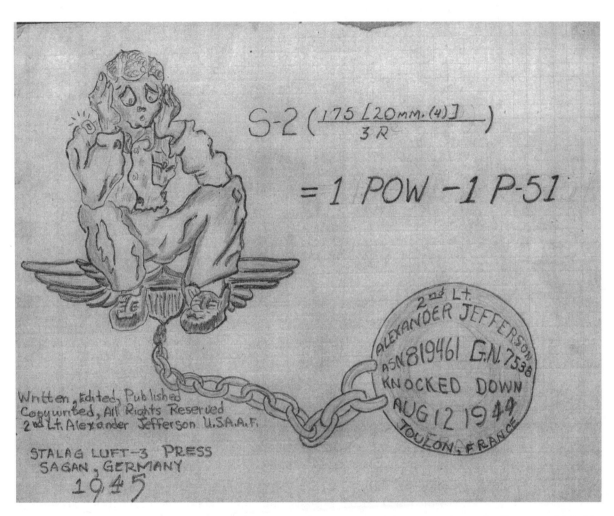

Kriegie Concept: S-2 represented Army Intelligence, multiplied by 175 20mm guns with four barrels, divided by the Third Reich, which equals one Prisoner of War, minus one P-51 Mustang.

Two World War II dates live in infamy for me. The first, December 7, 1941, I share with all my fellow citizens. The second is much more personal. On August 12, 1944, I was a proud member of the 332nd Fighter Group, later known as the Tuskegee Airmen. I was flying my P-51 on a strafing run over southern France. It was my nineteenth and final mission.

For the next nine months, I was a guest of the Third Reich. Actually, I was a *Kriegie*, which stands for *Kriegsgefangener* (prisoner of war). I was not held prisoner as long as many others were, but conditions were sufficiently challenging that I needed a diversion to keep my mind occupied. I started drawing the sketches that appear throughout this book after my arrival in Stalag Luft III on August 20, 1944, and I continued drawing them until we were liberated from Stalag VIIA on April 29, 1945. Because no cameras were available, I hoped that my drawings, which I drew on pale, yellow paper supplied by the International Red Cross, would document both my combat experiences as a fighter pilot and the frustrations that I endured as a prisoner of war.

My love of drawing and flying went back to my earliest years. In fact, I cannot remember a time when I was not drawing or making model airplanes. The smell of model plane glue still permeates my senses. I put together every known model imaginable. My masterpiece was a Supermarine Spitfire with twin two-foot floats and a three-foot wingspan. I drew the plans from newspaper photos. One of my most disheartening moments came in 1945. I had just arrived home from overseas, only to discover that my parents had thrown away my Supermarine Spitfire and all my modeling tools.

As a boy, I was also fascinated by a buck-toothed, rule-breaking, daredevil World War I pilot named Phineas Pinkham, who was always in some kind of trouble when he wasn't shooting down German planes. I read about his breath-taking exploits and those of other fighter pilots in a magazine called *Flying Aces*, and I dreamed of the day I would be performing my own heroic deeds.

By the time I arrived at Stalag Luft III, it had become a camp primarily for captured British and American Air Force officers. It was located just south of Sagan, approximately 90 miles southeast of Berlin in what is now southwestern Poland. The Luftwaffe administered the camp, and we were not overtly mistreated. As a result, many of my sketches appear lighthearted, even whimsical, but life for a prisoner was never that easy. It was simply too dangerous for me to draw a German sentry taking a shot at a POW reaching for a ball that had rolled under the warning wire, or a guard shooting and killing a prisoner who was standing in the doorway of his barracks. It was equally difficult, if not impossible, to sketch what it meant to stand for hours in subzero weather while the guards searched our barracks for *Kriegie* contraband or the endless hours of unmitigated hunger and boredom and those interminable nights spent longing for loved ones whom we were never quite sure we would see again.

While I was a prisoner, I also wrote down observations in a small notebook that, toward the end of my incarceration, became a running log on what was happening to us, especially after we were forced to evacuate Stalag Luft III and make the long trek to Stalag VIIA in Moosburg, Germany. Without these notations, there is no way that I could have recalled the many details of that bitterly cold march and our final days before liberation.

I began writing this memoir in 1948 when I became an elementary school science teacher in Detroit. Aviation was the general theme of my classroom, and I had several model planes hanging from the ceiling. When these 10- and 11-year-old black kids asked me, "Mr. Jefferson, what did you do during the war?", I would tell them, "I was there." Then I would describe how I felt living the life of a raunchy, daredevil fighter pilot and what it was like to be a "Negro" U.S. Army Air Corps pilot in these United States between 1943 and 1946. Over the ensuing decades, I continued to write down my recollections. Now I am in my ninth decade, and it is time to finish the job.

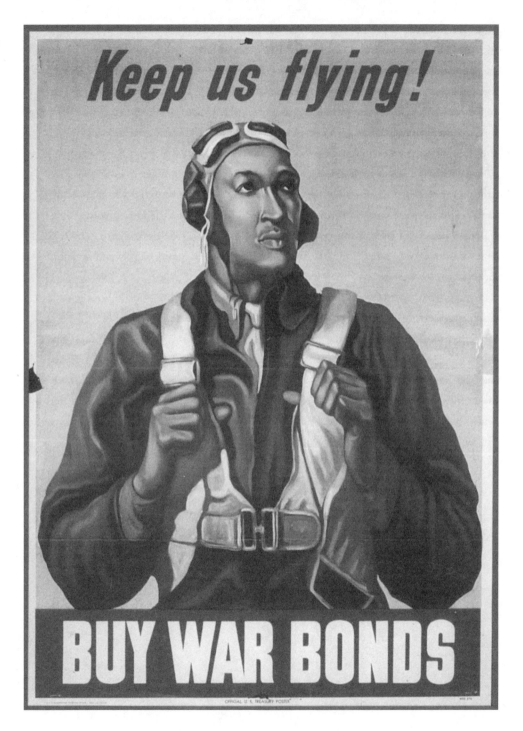

Tuskegee Airman Buy War Bonds poster.

1 **Detroit** The Formative Years

I was born in Detroit, Michigan, on November 15, 1921, the first child of Alexander Jefferson and Jane White Jefferson. My parents had only recently moved to Detroit from Atlanta, Georgia, because there were factory jobs to be had in the Motor City. They would have two more children: my sister, Emma, who was born on March 25, 1925, and my brother, Clarence, born on November 7, 1930.

My mother was born in 1891 in Newnan, Georgia, just southwest of Atlanta, into a prominent family that had long made its mark in religious and educational circles. Her paternal grandfather, William Jefferson White, was born in the 1830s to a slave woman and a white man, but he was never a slave. He became a minister of the Springfield Baptist Church in Augusta, Georgia, where in 1867, he opened a school in the church basement that he called Augusta Institute. This small, black, all-male school, which initially trained its students exclusively for the ministry and pedagogy, later moved to Atlanta. Over the years, it changed its name to Atlanta Baptist Seminary, Atlanta Baptist College, and finally, early in the twentieth century, Morehouse College. Today, Morehouse is a nationally and internationally respected liberal arts and medical school that offers a wide variety of majors to students from more than 40 states and 18 foreign countries. Dr. Martin Luther King, Jr. is one of Morehouse's most famous graduates.

Alexander Jefferson, age six months.

William Jefferson White had two families. One was legitimate, while the other, shall we say, existed in a backroom. I don't know much about the background of this second family, except that the woman in the backroom, who was a slave and seamstress in the master's house, gave birth to my grandfather, Henry Montgomery White, who became a very prominent Atlanta clergyman, and with whom I lived during my undergraduate college days. After Henry graduated in 1880 from Clark

Alexander Jefferson, age two years.

University, and later completed his studies at Gammon Theological Seminary, he became pastor of the South Atlanta Methodist Church, which is now known as the Henry Montgomery White United Methodist Church. His wife, Emma Nelson White, graduated from Atlanta University in 1885, and their daughter, Jane, became my mother.

Of course, we have no birth certificate, but we know that when my Grandfather White died in 1954, he was more than 100 hundred years old. When he lay on his deathbed, my mother remembers him ranting deliriously, reliving the horror of seeing his mother beaten by the master because she was somehow to blame when he and the master's son got into some type of trouble. At the time, the two boys were only 12 or 13. The master had evidently become so angry that he tied her hands, suspended her from a rafter in the barn, and whipped her.

My mother graduated from Clark in 1910 with a degree in pedagogy, which consisted of the art, methods, and principles of the teaching profession. She then taught school in Newnan until she married my father in 1920. Her two sisters, Lydia and Dorothy, were also graduates of Clark. Their parents stressed the importance of education, which would enable them to escape domestic service in a white man's household where they would be subject to mental and physical abuse.

Although Grandfather White had his college and seminary degrees, and Grandmother Emma White was also a college graduate, they did not encourage any of their four sons—Henry, Jr., Maceo, Charles, and Walter—to pursue higher education. Instead, they were encouraged to pursue manual trades as carpenters, mechanics, and handymen.

My father was born on March 25, 1880, near Lynchburg, in central South Carolina. His father, Fortune Jefferson, had been born a slave in 1832, which means that I am only two generations removed from slavery on both sides of my family. Fortune Jefferson was a very prolific man. My father was the tenth of 11 children. His mother, Susan Boone Jefferson, died giving birth to her twelfth child in 1890. Fortune then married 17-year-old Rosa Lee Thomas and proceeded to have seven more children. He ran a blacksmith shop in Lynchburg until he died in 1911.

There was nothing for a young black man to do around Lynchburg except share-cropping, so in 1916, my father left to seek employment in Atlanta, where he met my mother. Two years later, he went to Detroit and secured a job as a laborer at the Detroit Lubricator Company, which was owned by a black man named Eliza McCoy. My father worked for Detroit Lubricator the rest of his life, and although he joined the union, he remained a staunch Republican, simply because, he said, "They freed the slaves."

My father returned to Atlanta in 1920 to marry my mother, after which they immediately returned to Detroit. My father finished only the eighth grade, but he was a whiz with mathematical figures. I remember him sitting in his wooden rocker behind our isinglass stove and the orange peel aroma of Prince Albert tobacco rising from his pipe and filling the entire house. He would sit for hours, his lap filled with papers, systematically rotating, adding, subtracting, and manipulating numbers until finally he produced what he considered "the number" for the day, which he often hit.

Mother was a rigid moralist. As the product of a Methodist minister father and a university-educated mother, she was a real "MK" (minister's kid) and always very proper. She did not dance, and she drank nothing stronger than lemonade. But she was also an intellectual who had been greatly influenced by the professors at Clark University, where, among other things, she had studied Greek and Latin.

Dad, on the other hand, was very, very different. At least before they married, he loved to dance and have a good time. He was also a sharp dresser and enjoyed an occasional drink, although he had to keep his bottle of gin out in the barn. I discovered this only after I returned from the service, and he took me out back and offered me a drink to welcome me home!

My mother did not know that he played the numbers. A couple of times per week, he would secretly risk a few pennies with Keyser, the numbers man, a young Polish guy who lived right behind us. I'm not sure, but I think the payoff was 500 to 1, which meant for every penny bet, one might win five dollars.

My father was extremely hard working. During the long years of the Depression, he was fortunate to be the only man on our entire block who had a job. I can still see him walking home from the Buchanan Street trolley, swinging his lunch pail and greeting all the neighbor men on their front steps and them responding, "Hi, Mr. Jefferson."

(left)
Jane White Jefferson,
mother.
(right)
Alexander Jefferson,
father.

My father was also an unofficial "railroad conductor" for many of our relatives in the 1920s and 1930s who came north from Lynchburg, South Carolina, and Atlanta, looking for better lives. I can remember a steady stream of aunts and uncles moving me out of my bed and onto a cot or a wood pallet on the floor and having to run down to the corner store to get more groceries. My father was their financial support until they could find work and secure their own place to rent.

My father also took an interest in certain political figures, such as the Jamaican-born Marcus Garvey, who supported Black Nationalism and Pan-Africanism. My uncle John Fields was involved in the Congress of Industrial Organizations (CIO, which began in 1935) and which sometimes included confrontations with the local police.

Our address in Detroit was 4014 28th Street, and initially the house consisted of two side-by-side "shotgun" units. We lived in the north unit of four rooms. The front room was the parlor, which featured our piano. The next room was Mom and Dad's bedroom. One step down was my bedroom, and another step down was the kitchen, with a corner blocked off for the toilet. The sink was on the other side of the toilet, facing the stove. In back was our barn, one side of which had room for a car, and the other side contained bins for coal and coke.

Aunt Mame and Uncle Gee lived in the four-room unit on the other side of us. When they moved out in 1926, Dad cut two doors through the wall, so we then had an eight-room house. Our old kitchen became the bathroom, our parlor became Mom and Dad's bedroom, their bedroom became my sister Emma's bedroom, the room opposite my bedroom became the dining room, and in the room opposite Emma's bedroom was a large isinglass baseburner stove that heated the front six rooms.

One of my earliest memories of that house is the smell of boiling coffee at 4:00 a.m. Then I'd hear my father slam the door, and I'd go back to sleep. A couple of hours later, I faced the stark reality of getting up, washing my face in cold water, and eating shredded wheat with cold milk, even on the coldest winter days. But we never went hungry, and we never ate plain hamburger. Mr. Parsons, who was the owner and butcher at the corner store, would cut off strips of tenderloin and grind it for us. I thought that T-bone steak was part of a regular meal. There was sawdust on the store floor, and on the counter were huge jars of pickles and open spice containers that gave off a rich aroma. I remember Mr. Parsons scooping peanut butter out of a large tub into a paper container. The oil would leak through, and in a few days, the peanut butter would be as hard as a brick.

Then there was the C. F. Smith Bakery, where I would go to buy bread. It was about 10 blocks away on West Grand Boulevard, just south of Michigan Avenue, under the railroad viaduct. I could smell the heavenly aroma of the ovens the entire 10 blocks. Bread was then five cents per loaf, uncut and fresh out of the oven. I'd sometimes buy an extra loaf, scoop out the inside, and just eat the crust! Fantasti-cally delicious! No one today would dream of allowing a seven- or eight-year-old to walk up Jackson Street to the Boulevard, go under the railroad tracks, then onto Michigan Avenue.

One of our summer rituals was to fill several open-mouthed gallon jugs with peaches and then cover them with sugar. We would put the jugs next to the chimney, where the heat would proceed to do its duty. We were always told that the "juice" was a home remedy for medicinal purposes, such as winter coughs and colds. I do know it sure tasted good!

When the weather turned really cold, we heated bricks next to the baseburner and put them under the blankets of our beds. The blankets were heavy, wool army blankets or comforters made by my mother from odd pieces of old clothing. The kitchen stove was a combination coal and wood stove, with a warmer on top. Food must have been different back then because sweet potatoes stayed in the warmer day and night and never spoiled. The wood and coal stove kept the kitchen and dining room warm. There was also a gas heater with a door that you had to open and ignite the gas with a match. I recall forgetting to turn off the gas one day, and the tank overheated and almost burst.

Coal was then $4 per ton and was delivered directly through the alley to the coal bins in the barn. I was often responsible for directing the deliveryman to put the coal into the correct bin. Coke went into one bin, used at night to bank the fire, and hard coal went into the other bin. If they got mixed, I caught hell. It was also my responsibility to carry the coal into the house in a scuttle and to take out the ashes in the morning and evening. I dumped the ashes in the backyard. In the spring, we turned the ashes into the soil and raised the biggest and best collards you have ever seen.

Dish Night was a big event in our neighborhood. To get your free dish, you went to the Buchanan Theater on Friday night and on Saturday to the Crystal Theater on Michigan Avenue. The price of admission was a nickel, and for this, you received a piece of pottery or cutlery. Of course, we would also catch up on the newsreels and the latest Mickey Mouse cartoons. Sometimes the Crystal would offer two dishes for the price of one admission. Much of our everyday dinnerware came from these two theaters.

My parents never owned an automobile or learned to drive. We traveled by bus or streetcar. I didn't own a store-bought shirt until I got in the army. My mother made my shirts as well as my sister's clothes. I ironed my own clothes. I also helped with the canning of fruits and vegetables and with the baking and quilt making.

The Detroit of my youth was very conservative and very safe. Doors were left unlocked, but we kids never had free reign in the neighborhood. If I did something wrong, the neighbors were not above punishing me. Of course, news of what I had done got back home faster than I did, so when I got back home, I could expect even more trouble because whatever I had done was an insult to my family's reputation.

We lived in a Polish neighborhood, except for the occasional Jewish family. The majority of these Poles were from the old country, and one of my fondest memories is the delicious potato pancakes they used to make. Our next-door neighbor to the south was the Wonokowski family, and to the north lived the Jankowski family. The Jankowskis had a boy my age named Jiggs and an older brother, Phil, who always kept his right hand in his pocket because he had injured it working at Kelsey Hayes. They also had two girls: Eleanor was a tomboy, who played baseball in the alley better than any boy, and Cecelia, whom we knew as "See Law."

The Polish youngsters attended St. Hedwich, which was the local Polish Catholic church. I'm not sure what we thought of the Catholic religion. I do know that I never attended church with them or they with me. I also sensed that their parents did not completely approve of my sister and me. After years of living side by side, Mrs. Jankowski revealed, somewhat apologetically in her broken English, that her priest had instructed her never to have anything to do with "colored" people. The Jankowskis were very, very poor. I was astonished when the children came out of the house with a piece of bread, smeared with lard and sprinkled with sugar. They considered this a once-a-week treat. An orange, they told me, was something you looked forward to only at Christmas.

The Poles referred to a Jewish man who lived two blocks away on Jackson Street, between Lovett and Scotten, as "the Sheenie Man." He rode a horse-drawn wagon through the alleys, picking up and buying junk. I saw the hatred and resentment the Poles felt for him, but this Sheenie Man educated both sons to become doctors.

When I was 13 or 14, I worked for the Sheenie Man for about a year. He had a Model T truck, and I got the job of driving it up and down the alleys. We scavenged or bought copper wire, aluminum pots and pans, paper, iron, and steel. Burning the insulation off the copper wire was my job, and the smell of that acrid smoke still comes to my nostrils whenever I think of him.

A very fair "colored" woman named Mrs. Clark lived across the street from us. Her equally light-skinned husband walked every morning to the streetcar line dressed in coat, shirt, and tie, and carrying a small satchel. He was said to have a job as a barber in a downtown hotel. We never considered them to be Negroes because they lived apart from us until their grandson came to visit. His name was Martin Jenkins, and years later, he helped me get into graduate school at Howard University.

My mother had an extensive library. I recall sitting on the floor completely engrossed in the wooden engraved illustrations I found in *Les Misérables*. I also remember reading to myself at a very young age. Daily newspapers were a very important part of the daily routine in our house, and my sister and I always fought over the funnies, until my dad insisted that we read the headlines to him. I thought that was kind of lazy of him, but it became a fascinating game. He would wait until I had read several headlines, and then ask me, "What was the second headline? Don't look!"

School was always easy for me and never much of a challenge. I was double-promoted twice in elementary school. I went to kindergarten at the old Newberry Elementary School a block away, in a structure that was built about 1895. Then, while the new Newberry School was being constructed, I walked to the first grade at Craft Elementary on Vinewood and Michigan Avenues, approximately two miles from our house.

My third-grade teacher, Mrs. Laidlaw, gave me hell. To avoid her wrath, I always finished my lessons before anyone else, so she didn't know what to do with me. My sixth-grade teacher, Mrs. Simpson, was an austere, unsmiling disciplinarian. Try as I might, I could never outmaneuver her. She was always one step ahead of me, and I learned to appreciate and respect her. I know she was responsible for greatly improving my English.

As the oldest child in the family and being male, I was aware at a very early age that I was a Negro. I remember going downtown to Hudson's Department Store with my mother when I was five or six and noticing that the only blacks working there were very fair-skinned women. They held the auspicious position of elevator operators and wore black uniforms with lacy white aprons. I also knew there were restaurants in Detroit that did not serve blacks. My mother introduced me to this fact by saying, "We can't stop here," and I somehow understood that the reason was our color.

I also had to walk home from school through "foreign" territory, which meant Polish or Jewish. There were often racial slurs and indignities, and one thing would lead to another. This meant I either had to run or pick up a two-by-four or a rock or use my fists and fight my way home. Nevertheless, until I was in my teens, I was accepted by the Polish boys in my immediate neighborhood. They would even fight to protect me when we ventured out of the neighborhood.

We were the 28th Street Gang, and I was the only black member. I still remember some of their "names": Frenchie was my age; Keyser, who lived behind us on Jackson Street, was several years older and ran the numbers; Bed Bug lived up the block from us; Jiggs lived next door; then there was Horse's Ass. Our activities ranged from standing around doing nothing to playing baseball, making tree houses, baking potatoes in a cardboard playhouse, and deliberately intruding on the territory of the 30th Street Gang, which almost always resulted in a running fight.

We also challenged other street gangs, such as the Bangor Street and the 31st Street gangs. We looked forward to these confrontations. If a fight broke out, we fought with rocks, fists, and Coke bottles, but never with knives or firearms. I must admit I had very good speed and was also very adept at jumping fences!

On one occasion, we ventured about six blocks north and were chased home by the Warren Avenue Gang, which was all black. Interestingly, the only other contact I had with blacks occurred on Sunday mornings when we went to Scott Methodist Episcopal Church at St. Antoine and Kirby Streets. Both the church and street are long gone, paved over by the urban renewal project that became I-75. Scott Church was a large wooden structure sitting right on the sidewalk. Dad sang in the choir. As a three- or four-year-old, I remember following him up the wooden stairs, past the wainscoted panels, and up into the choir loft. Scott Church was the social and religious center of our lives. At that time, young people's organizations like the Boy Scouts and the Boys Club drew the color line. There was a Boys Club only eight blocks from my home, but I was not allowed inside. Detroit had one YMCA exclusively for blacks and another one that allowed us to use its facilities, but both were located in the ghetto on the lower east side of the city.

We kids knew all the police who cruised our neighborhood in open four-door roadsters, which we called The Big Four. We would shoot craps on the corner of 28th and Jackson, furtively watching for cops, and, when sighted, we would grab the dice and money and run like hell! Sometimes the cops won, and they would threaten us. They would usually give us back our dice, but never the money! Despite all the trouble we caused, I was never manhandled by the police, who were always white. I had the strange feeling that if I had been anywhere else than 40 feet from my front door and a known member of the community and the gang, things might have been different.

I also knew I would not have been so fortunate if something like this had happened in the South. Every summer, we traveled to Atlanta to visit my grandfather.

One time, when I was maybe 12 or 13, my grandfather sent me to the corner store. I went in and announced, "I want a nickel's worth of bologna and five cents worth of grits." The indignant owner angrily said, "What did you say, boy?" When I repeated my order, he said, "Don't you know how to speak to me, boy?" I told him, "Hell, no." Fortunately, my grandfather was "the Methodist minister" for black Atlanta, so there were no repercussions for him, although he immediately shipped me home to Detroit because I had been so disrespectful. When I was in fourth or fifth grade, I began skipping school and walking some three miles to a small airfield on the corner of Ford Road and Wyoming. I would hang around, doing odd jobs and helping the mechanics work on planes. I also got my first ride in a bi-winged plane that I believe was a Waco. If my mother had known this, she would have killed me.

When I was about 11, something happened that made me realize I wanted to stay in school. I had become totally uninvolved with my schoolwork because I was bored and unchallenged. Then, one day, my father forgot his lunch, and I had to take it to him at the Detroit Lubricator Company. The walk to the foundry, which was located on Marquette and Trumble Streets, was only a couple of miles, but it was summer, and the weather was sticky and hot, probably in the 90s. As I walked into the factory, I was curious about the owner, Elijah McCoy, whom my father had once described as "a Negro man who walks around the plant with an air and is respected wherever he goes." Much later, I learned that Elijah McCoy had been born to fugitive slaves in Canada in the 1840s. He had studied mechanical engineering in Scotland before settling near Ypsilanti, Michigan after the Civil War. In 1872, he invented an automatic oiler for the wheels and axles of steam engines. When competitors came up with their own inferior versions, train engineers demanded "The Real McCoy." McCoy subsequently moved to Detroit, where he opened the factory where my father worked. When he died in the late 1920s, he held more than 40 patents on various mechanical devices.

Of course, I didn't know any of this on that hot summer day, and I certainly did not see Mr. McCoy when I walked into his factory and asked one of his workers where I could find my father. "Oh, yeah," he said, "Jeff's back in the foundry."

When I reached the foundry, the stifling heat, humidity, and odor hit me in the face, and I almost passed out. My dad was stripped to the waist, sweating like a hog, holding one end of a ladle, with another man on the other end. My dad weighed

Foundry, Detroit.

about 145 pounds, but he was all muscle. The two of them were pouring molten aluminum into sand castings to make carburetors. Seeing my father slaving under those conditions made me swear to myself, "God, if you let me get out of here, I'll never go into a foundry again the rest of my life."

Foundries at that time had no showers or locker rooms for changing clothes. My father had to travel on the streetcar, summer or winter, out of that foundry into the cold or heat. He went through at least four bouts with pneumonia, and the last one finished him. He died in 1954 due to complications of silicosis and pneumonia. X-rays showed that his lungs looked like the black branches of a tree. He was 74.

Strangely enough, I grew up feeling isolated from my two siblings. Emma was five years younger than I, and Clarence was nine years my junior; consequently, growing up we had little in common. While I was out running the streets, Emma was inside with my mother, doing "girls'" work. She entered Clark in September of the year I graduated. She married in 1950, and that same year I finally realized I also had a brother when he began babysitting my daughter, Alexis Louise. Later, we became fishing buddies, and, over the years, all three of us grew very close.

My seventh and eighth grades were spent at Condon Intermediate School at West Grand Boulevard and Buchanan. I transferred to Munger Intermediate for ninth grade in order to take the college preparatory course, which included Latin and college algebra. My determined mother had to have a confrontation with the principal of Condon to expedite this change. Munger Intermediate was located on Martin and McGraw Streets, next to Chadsey High School, which I also attended.

When I was in ninth grade at Munger, I experienced an incident that really angered me. I don't remember the exact language, but my English teacher, a Mrs. Stellberger, made a covertly racist remark that I took personally. In retaliation, I called her a "left-handed shit-grabber." My mother and I had to attend a command conference with the teacher, the counselor, and the principal in order to keep me in school. When the incident was reconstructed, an audible silence came over the room. Mrs. Stellberger and I met again in 1958. She was in the Detroit Federation of Teachers Building stuffing envelopes for the union when I walked in. She looked at me across the table and exclaimed, "Alexander Jefferson! What are you doing here?" I guess it was no surprise that she remembered me.

I had weaned myself away from the 28th Street Gang by the time I began Chadsey High School. Simply put, we were going in different directions. I knew I was going on to college, but my Polish friends and their parents considered finishing high school and going to work in a factory to be the epitome of success.

My years at Chadsey were uneventful except for the intensity of my interest in chemistry and biology and the hours spent in the laboratories. I took great pleasure in drawing the specimens we studied in biology, especially the entrails of a dissected frog. As for the rest of my classes, I passively endured them, satisfied just to receive passing grades. I remember many of these courses were simply too easy, and I became bored. So I entertained myself designing and drawing airplanes, multifaceted constellations, and all kinds of ships and cars. I do not recall anyone at the school counseling or criticizing me for not doing better in these classes.

There were only a few black students in my Chadsey graduation class of 1938, and none in my college prep classes. The other blacks came from American Street, north of Warren Avenue, in the opposite direction from my home. I never really had any contact with them. I also had little contact with my white classmates outside the classroom. There were never any after-school social functions where I would have felt welcome. For this same reason, I did not attend my senior prom. After all, with whom would I have danced? So going through school, I was pretty much a loner, spending most of my school time in the biology and chemistry laboratories.

There were other racial indignities in the Detroit of my youth. I knew that certain clubs and most neighborhoods were not open to blacks. I also knew that blacks were not allowed to ride the *SS Tashmoo*, which was the excursion boat on the Detroit River on which my high school class held its graduation party. But the most unconscionable incident of racism that I experienced in Michigan occurred several years later, in May 1944. I was then a young second lieutenant in the U.S. Air Corps, and several of us attempted to integrate the whites only Officers Club at Selfridge Field, just outside Detroit. It was a humiliating experience, but it was all part of my growing up in mid–twentieth century America.

2 Clark College

Alexander Jefferson, college senior, 1942.

There was never any question about my attending college, and I had long known that it would be Clark College, founded in 1869 by the Freedmen's Aid Society of the Methodist Episcopal Church, which later became the United Methodist Church. When I started college in 1938, Clark was still known as Clark University, but after it moved in 1941 to downtown Atlanta, across the street from Atlanta University and Morehouse College, it became Clark College. In 1988, the official name became Clark Atlanta University.

I find it odd that today so many young people have to be motivated and pushed into college. I took it for granted that college was just part of the process of growing up. Grandfather White, my mother, and her two sisters were all graduates of Clark, so going to Clark College was a given. I would, of course, stay with Grandfather and "Mother," who was his second wife.

I even had my own car to drive to Atlanta. In 1937, my mother's brother Mace, who had moved to Detroit, had given her a 1932 Model A Ford coupe, with a rumble seat and big wire-spoked wheels. Unfortunately, no one in my family drove, so it was put up on blocks in our barn, where it stayed until the following summer, when after my graduation from high school, I was given permission to drive it. I had to clear the junk from around it, remove the blocks, pump up the tires by hand, put in oil and gas, and recharge the battery. Imagine my exuberance when, after many bruised knuckles, that four-cylinder motor coughed and began to chug!

I drove Lizzie all alone to Atlanta that fall of 1938, but I already knew the road and what to expect. Every summer, my mother's brother-in-law, Norman, would drive four or five of us in his car to visit Grandfather White. Because there were few if any restaurants that would feed us after we crossed the Mason-Dixon Line, we would pack enough fried chicken and other food for the entire trip. There was also no place

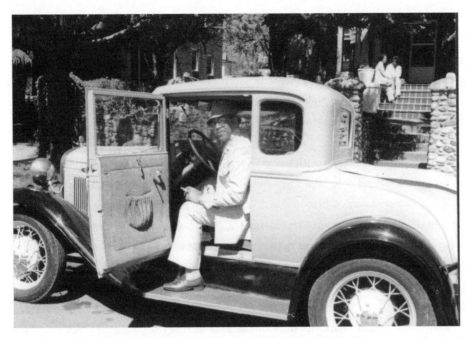

where we were allowed to stay overnight, so we'd drive straight through to Atlanta. It was about 800 miles, and we'd make it in something less than 24 hours. Uncle Norman knew where we could stop to buy gasoline and find a bathroom.

So when I set out on my own, I knew exactly what to do. I had enough money to buy gas and sufficient chicken to snack on, and that was pretty much it. I remember between Lexington and Chattanooga following a Greyhound bus around those dangerous mountain curves on old, two-lane US 25. But Lizzie and I navigated those roads, and we arrived in Atlanta with no problems.

I moved into Grandfather White's house on the south side of Atlanta, just two blocks from Clark College. Grandfather was then the pastor emeritus of the South Atlanta Methodist Church. He was in his late 80s or early 90s and almost blind, but he was still performing hard physical labor. My grandfather owned eight or nine shotgun houses that he rented out, and it was a full-time job to keep them in repair. I remember being with him on a two-story roof and him saying, "Alex, give me a nail! Now, show me where it goes?" I'd place his hand on the spot; he'd feel it with his finger, place the nail, and pound it in. He did this while sitting on the edge of the roof, with his feet hanging over the edge, and me hanging onto the top of the ladder, trying to keep him from slipping off.

Helping him, I learned how to mix red mud, cement, and lime to make plaster for walls. I also learned how to repair toilets with used plumbing materials; patch roofs with makeshift paper and cardboard; mix concrete with sand, gravel, lime, and a little cement; and fix rotting windows and porches. You name it, Grandpa could repair it. At the time, I weighed 110 pounds dripping wet, and when we used a big crosscut saw to cut up crossties for the fireplace, I can still hear him yelling, "Pull that saw, boy! Don't push it!"

I loved eating breakfast with my grandfather because it was so different from the shredded wheat and cold milk I was used to at home. I would wake up to the wonderful aroma of grits, gravy, biscuits, and pork chops. And if I needed something to eat later in the day, I could stop at the corner drug store and buy a pig ear sandwich for a nickel. A boiled pig ear slapped between a couple of slices of bread and covered with lots of mustard and relish was simply delicious. I'd top that off with a Coke that was much stronger than anything we drink today. Coca-Cola really was Coca-Cola back in those days.

I have many fond memories of South Atlanta during my college years. First, there was the wonderful relationship I had with Lizzie. We drove around together for five years, interrupted only by the nine months when I was undergoing my pilot training at Tuskegee Army Airfield. We spent three years on the old campus at Clark and one at the new campus, which was located in the inner city across from Morehouse College. Owning a car made me a Big Man on Campus. A couple of guys rode with me every day to the new campus, and each gave me a nickel for gas. Lizzie and I were also on the cheerleading squad at Clark. I was too light to play football and too short for basketball, but we cheerleaders had great fun climbing in Lizzie and following the teams to the away games.

I was always very conscious of the fact I was a "Northern Negro." Because of this and my dark complexion and lack of involvement in politically active campus organizations, I was not accepted into the socially exclusive Alpha Phi Alpha fraternity, which took great pride that its members were "light, bright, and damn near white."

I did just fine without fraternity life because I spent most of my time at Clark in the labs or on dates. Lizzie and I often drove our ladies into the city or the surrounding countryside; in fact, I seem to recall two or three very nice, secluded lovers' lanes!

Clark's move to its new campus in the center of Atlanta greatly affected student life. Everything seemed in turmoil. New buildings were going up everywhere, traffic was heavy, and the pace of life was more hectic. We Clark males entered into gentlemanly competition for our co-eds with our counterparts at Morehouse, which was an all-male school. And the males from both schools competed for the girls of Spelman College, which was a girls' school just down the street. Atlanta University was no threat because its graduate students were older and much more serious. God, did we have fun!

I majored in chemistry and biology and minored in physics and math. I was badgered but sustained by Professor Brooks, a light-skinned Jamaican. His wife, Stella Brooks, was head of the English Department and a virtual dictator. For 30 years, she remained the bulwark of the English departments at Clark College and Atlanta University. I flunked her English course because, I now realize, I resented her autocratic attitude. But ironically, 10 years later, I grew to respect, revere, and embrace her holy trinity of grammar, rhetoric, and punctuality, upon which she stood and from which she refused to be moved.

I was in the Philharmonic Society and the Clark Choir, led by the one and only J. DeKoven Killingsworth, a left-handed, cockeyed, strawberry-splotched, red-haired, straight-fingered musical genius. You could never tell in which direction he was looking. Between long hours in the chemistry, biology, and physics labs and my many soirées with Lizzie around Atlanta and its surrounding countryside, I often barely made rehearsals on time. We frequently went on tour, performing in black churches in such fascinating cities as Washington, Philadelphia, Cleveland, Chicago, St. Louis, and Memphis. We traveled by bus, and the girls were very well chaperoned. I sang first bass in the male quartet, and during every concert, the audience always requested us to sing two or three spirituals.

Life on the original Clark College campus was a wonderful experience. It was situated in the midst of 100 acres of serene woods. This isolation meant we didn't come in contact with racism unless, of course, we went off campus, where everything was segregated, even the water fountains. We were forced to sit at the back of buses and streetcars, but in the front car of trains, right behind the soot and steam of the engines. The campus of Georgia Tech was off-limits to persons of color, and we were not allowed to try on clothes at Riches Department Store in downtown Atlanta. We could go to the movie theaters, but we had to sit in the balcony. The theater we most frequented in Atlanta was the Fox. We bought our tickets at the front box office, but then had to walk around to the side of the building and climb a long steel stairway to the balcony.

Even the parks were segregated. We played our homecoming football game with archrival Morris Brown College at Ponce de Leon Park. Normally, this park was off-limits to us, but for this auspicious annual event, the city allowed us to use it. The city even ran streetcars to the campus gate. The students would board and ride up Capital Avenue, through downtown Atlanta, and then out to Ponce de Leon Park for our grand celebration. All of black Atlanta would turn out. Of course, I loaded up Lizzie with the female cheerleaders, and we escorted the streetcars and other vehicles with great fanfare. I can still see that 1932 roadster, with its big balloon tires and wire spokes, its rumble seat filled with those cute cheerleaders, honking its way to Ponce de Leon Park for the big game. Except for the driver, it was a reputed fact that Lizzie never carried a "hard leg," which refers to the male of the species. Atlanta was then a dry city, so we also carried with us our sweet syrupy Southern Comfort, mixed in Coke bottles, and a good time was had by all!

This marvelously carefree undergraduate life ended for me at 10:30 on the morning of June 2, 1942, when my class became the first to graduate from the new campus. After the formal ceremony, there was no great celebration. I recall no graduation pictures, dances, or parties. It was simply time to leave, so I packed up Lizzie and headed home to Detroit.

3 The Making of a Tuskegee Airman

It was June, 1942, there was a war on, and I was back home in Detroit after my graduation from Clark. I knew I was going to be drafted, but I had high hopes I would be able to join the Army Air Corps. Actually, blacks had been fighting for the right to join the Air Corps since World War I. Finally, on April 3, 1939, Public Law 18 called for an expansion of the Air Corps, including the authorization of programs in black colleges to train African Americans for Air Corps support services. Then, on January 16, 1941, the War Department contracted with Tuskegee Institute to train black pilots for what would become the 99th Fighter Squadron. This was during my junior year at Clark, so when recruiters came on campus to sign up volunteers, I immediately wrote home asking permission to join. Although I was then old enough to sign up without parental permission, my dad very emphatically said, "Hell, no! If you were meant to fly, you would've been born with wings. Now, finish college!" It was the first time I had ever heard the old man swear. As a dutiful son, I complied.

I had always wanted to fly, and my hobby of building model airplanes had continued even during my college days. I clearly remembered Lindbergh's flight across the Atlantic, the Great Zeppelin flying over Detroit, and the whole phenomena of flight during the late 1930s and early 1940s. I read every comic book and magazine that had anything to do with flight and constructed all kinds of model airplanes. I even drew the plans and built a model of a super English float plane with a 49-inch wing span. The actual plane had held the world speed record in 1933. I was so fascinated by planes that I even skipped grade school classes to go out to a small airport, where I washed planes and did other odd jobs for rides.

After Pearl Harbor, I knew that if I were drafted, I would end up as a buck private earning $21 per month in a segregated quartermaster company, forced to perform heavy, nasty, dirty work. But the life of a flying cadet meant $75 per month and a fancy uniform that was sure to attract beautiful women. After nine months, my pay would increase to $150 per month, plus $75 flying pay. I would also have my wings, and, with any luck, even more lovely ladies!

After I returned to Detroit, I went to the Federal Building and passed the written examination for the Army Air Corps with flying colors, but I flunked the physical. I weighed 116.5 pounds, and the minimum was 117. I was told to go downstairs, drink some water, and eat a couple of bananas. When I returned, I got on the scales and just made it. On September 23, 1942, I was sworn into the Army Reserves. I immediately volunteered for flight training but was told to return home and wait for a position to open up. When I asked when this would be, I was told not to worry about it. I wasn't sure I would ever be called, but at least being in the reserves kept me from being drafted. At the time, I didn't understand what was going on, but I later learned there was a rigid quota restricting how many blacks could be inducted each month into the training program at Tuskegee.

Disappointed, I returned to my old 28th Street neighborhood, only to find that it had greatly changed because of the war. Many of my old friends were already in the armed services. I didn't want just to sit around, so I got a job in a small steel-treating plant on East Six Mile. I worked as an analytical chemist, running carbon analysis tests on the steel that came out of the furnaces. Surprisingly, that job paid me twice as much as my father was then making as a laborer.

I held that job from about June 15 until the middle of September, 1942, when I had an unexpected opportunity to begin graduate school. I've already mentioned Mrs. Clark, who lived across the street from us. Her grandson, Martin Jenkins, who was 10 or 15 years older than I, was then on the faculty of Howard University in Washington, DC. When he came to Detroit that summer for a visit, we talked about graduate school. Through his efforts, I was accepted at Howard as a graduate student in the Chemistry Department. Martin Jenkins would later become president of Morgan State University in Baltimore.

I had long had an interest in chemistry. My mother had always insisted that I read, and she encouraged me to go to the local library, where, after spending countless hours thumbing through scientific textbooks and pamphlets, I decided I wanted to become a research chemist. I always knew I had the intellectual ability to accomplish whatever I wished, and if any doubts ever crept into my mind, the firm hand of my mother quickly dispelled them.

So, once again, I drove Lizzie off to school. In Washington, I shared a basement apartment on 6th Street with a guy named Cotton, right across the street from the chemistry building. To help defray my expenses, I taught a freshman class in organic chemistry. My life centered almost exclusively on that chemistry building. I have no memory of any other campus activities, not even of entering any other buildings on campus, except the library. The one professor who stands out in my mind was Dr. Sherashefsky, who had just returned from doing secret research for the government and had become very ill. Only later did I learn that his research dealt with the effects of radiation.

I rarely wandered off campus, and I never went downtown to visit the museums or other tourist attractions because wartime Washington was still a very racist city and completely segregated. The one section of the city I could and did occasionally visit was bordered by 7th Street, U Street, and Florida Avenue, located five or six blocks south of Howard University. On these fascinating and vibrant streets, I could come alive. I greatly enjoyed listening to the moving gospel music of the storefront churches on 7th Street, performed with tambourines, guitars, organs, and drums, and I found the jazz and blues played at the Baptist church equally compelling.

The cultural center for black Washington, however, was the Howard Theater, where every Friday night, when the venue changed, the first 10 rows were filled with Howard University students. All the great vaudeville stars and acts from the Chitlin' Circuit played the Howard Theater. I remember seeing Cab Calloway, Fats Waller, Duke Ellington, Count Basie, Chick Webb, Ella Fitzgerald, Billy Eckstein, Patterson and Jackson, and "Here Come Da Judge" Peg Leg Bates.

I never finished my first year at Howard because I received my orders to begin my flight training in April, 1943. The notice to report to the Tuskegee Army Airfield (TAAF) went to Detroit, and my family immediately notified me. I was so excited about having my class date that I immediately notified the Chemistry Department I was leaving school, and then drove Lizzie home to Detroit.

Once again, Lizzie went up on blocks in the barn, and I got ready to head south. When the C&O train left from the old train station on Michigan Avenue and 14th Street, I rode coach. In Cincinnati, however, I transferred to the Louisville and Nashville Line, which meant all blacks had to move to the first car behind the coal-burning steam engine. The South's discriminatory travel arrangements were not new to me, but it was still hard to endure the soot and hard seats. There were also no food or lavatory facilities for blacks, and the odor of urine was disgusting. But this was the way black soldiers went to war, at least in the South.

Chehaw Train Station, Alabama. Alexander Jefferson (l) with Chauncey E. Spencer, who promoted the Civilian Pilot Training Program for blacks, and Wardell Polk, a member of the 477th Bomber Group, who was arrested for protesting discriminatory policies in 1945.

In Atlanta, I again changed trains, and boarded one heading for Montgomery, Alabama. I remember the porter calling out such stops as Fairburn, LaGrange, and West Point, Georgia and then Opelika, Auburn, and finally Chehaw, Alabama, where nine or 10 of us future cadets got off.

It was ten o'clock at night, and we could see nothing except a small building about 100 yards away. As we walked toward it, we could make out the word "Chehaw" on the end. There was nothing else, no town, nothing. We had no idea what we were supposed to do, so we just stood there. Finally, a 6 × 6 army truck rolled up, and the driver told us to get in. At precisely eleven o'clock at night on April 13, 1943, we arrived at the Tuskegee Army Airfield to begin our training.

We cadets were all college graduates and highly motivated and aggressive. I look back now and realize to be black then and survive, you had to be that way. I think there were 90 of us who started in Class 44-A, so called because we were supposed to graduate in January, 1944. By the end of our nine months of training, only 25 of us had survived. Some were eliminated for flying inadequacies, and some for non-military reasons. Years later, through the Freedom of Information Act, we discovered there had been a quota for how many blacks were allowed to graduate. The phrase used to wash guys out was "eliminated while passing for the convenience of the government."

The night before graduation, all of us who had made it that far went to sleep, fully expecting to pin on our wings the next day. The next morning, however, we discovered that three or four members of our class had been pulled out and told they were not going to graduate. Some of them had even purchased their uniforms and invited their parents and sweethearts to come to graduation. It was a loss of their manhood, and it caused them a lot of psychological stress; in fact, some of them are still psychologically wounded because they were washed out. I know some of these guys could fly better than I could, and they were certainly better soldiers. Hell, I was a damned civilian, not a soldier.

The training itself was very challenging and very hectic. The specific details remain a blur as we worked our way through the stages of preflight, primary, basic, and advanced training. I do remember being harassed by the upperclassmen. We were the "Dummies," which meant we were supposed to be hazed. There was constant deep knee bending, duck walking, and sitting on an imaginary little red stool with your back braced against the wall, arms across your chest, and alternately kicking your

Air Cadet Alexander Jefferson.

feet out and back. We'd also be rousted in the middle of the night by upperclassmen, just in from night flying, who took great delight in ordering us to do our best imitation of a plane, "flying" up and down the hall with our arms outstretched.

I never took the hazing personally. I knew it was a way to weed out those who could not stand up under adverse stress or take direct and rigorous commands. There was no physical contact, just psychological abuse, which many men could not handle.

The one pleasant interlude was a glorious day between preflight and primary training when I returned to Atlanta and strutted through campus and my other old haunts, showing off the splendor of my new uniform. When I visited my old chemistry and biology labs, the freshmen and even the professors looked at me in awe.

On July 1, 1943, we completed our preflight training and moved on to primary, which was conducted on the campus of Tuskegee Institute. Our preflight training had consisted of three months of ground and flight training, which had been commercially farmed out to Tuskegee

Institute. The ground and flight instructors were black civilians. Chief Charles Alfred Anderson, who a few years earlier had taken Mrs. Eleanor Roosevelt for a plane ride to convince her that blacks could fly, was the supervisor of the flight instructors. In contrast, all instructors at the Tuskegee Army Airfield, where we took our basic and advanced training, were white regular army personnel.

I want to say something about Colonel Noel F. Parrish, the white, Southern-born commander of the Tuskegee Army Airfield when I went through training. In December, 1942, he had replaced Colonel Frederick Kimble, the first Tuskegee commander, who was much more interested in maintaining total segregation on base—including ordering white officers not to fraternize with their black cadets—than he was in training future pilots. Parrish himself was not a crusader for civil rights, but, unlike Kimble, he was determined that we should succeed. His father had been an itinerant minister in Kentucky, Georgia, and Alabama. Colonel Parrish had attended Rice Institute in Texas for a couple of years before enlisting. He eventually earned his commission and became a flight instructor in the Army Air Corps. His standards for us were every bit as high as for the white pilots he had previously trained. He insisted that anything less would get us killed, and he was quite willing to wash out anyone who did not perform up to his high expectations. Above all, he tried to stand up for us when many of his superiors wanted us to fail.

For our primary training, we were assigned rooms in the basement of a dormitory just inside the campus gate. My class and Class 43-J went through primary at the same time. My class included four other cadets from Michigan: Robert Cain, Leon Duncan Coleman, and Wardell Polk, all from Detroit, and Charles Walker from Jackson. We flew in the morning and attended classes in the afternoon. The other class did just the opposite. Classes were held in the building next to the dormitory in which we were staying. We ate in the mess hall across the square. I do not recall visiting any other buildings on campus because we were far too busy.

We did our early flying at Moton Field, which was five or six miles from the Tuskegee campus. It was a dirt field with a couple of large hangers, one of which had a tall parachute-training tower alongside it. For our primary training, we flew the Boeing Stearman PT-17, which was a tandem two-seater with two fabric-covered wings and an open cockpit. My instructor was Perry Young, a black civilian pilot from the Coffey School of Aeronautics, a private flight school at Harlem Airport on the south side of Chicago, where Cornelius R. Coffey and Willa Brown had first promoted aviation in the black community in the 1930s and 1940s.

I was the first in my class to solo, doing so after eight hours. Then I ground-looped, which meant that I landed too high, and when the wheels touched down, the plane veered off to the right, and the wing dragged the ground. This happened about six days before our class was scheduled to leave for basic training, but I passed my final check ride, and with the other survivors, returned to the Tuskegee Army Airfield for basic, where we flew the Vultee BT-13, which we called the "Vibrator."

Each class lost guys to accidents. I think we lost two men out of our class. We knew this happened in every class, but, as individuals, we figured it always happened to somebody else. We were young, and we considered ourselves invincible. I remember during primary training at Moton Field one morning, a B-26 came smoking in for a landing. All hell broke loose! The pilot had lost an engine on takeoff from TAAF about 10 miles away, and Moton Field was the closest field he could see. They had to truck the plane out because it was impossible to fly, but fortunately no one was hurt.

Another unforgettable sight was seeing and hearing a P-40 go straight in from high

Alexander Jefferson and his Class 44-A during advanced training at Tuskegee. Jefferson is standing fifth from the left.

altitude. It's very eerie to hear the piercing whine of a plane as it increases in speed, going straight in. The date was July 9, 1943, and Lieutenant Oscar Kenny lost his life.

After we moved from primary at Moton to TAAF for basic and then advanced training, there was still some hazing from upper classmen, but not nearly as much because we were now becoming upperclassmen, with Dummies below us whom we were supposed to help train. After all, our future life in combat might very well depend on them.

Advanced training was fascinating. Night cross-country trips were especially challenging. Once again, I ground-looped, this time in the BT-13, because I was careless and inattentive. My airspeed dropped below stall, and the plane fell in from 20 feet and bounced over on a wing. Nevertheless, I again passed my final check ride, this time with Gabe Hawkins, who was called Old Scar Face because of the scars he incurred when his face smashed into the instrument panel during a crash landing.

Graduation was an exciting day. My mother came down from Detroit, and my grandfather came from Atlanta, along with my sister, Emma, and our cousin, Gwendolyn, both of whom were attending Clark College. I was standing tall, dressed smart-

Alexander Jefferson and friend, Gwen Austin, at club in Washington, DC, while on leave in 1944.

ly in my "pinks and greens," with my new wings proudly attached to my chest. It was an exhilarating experience for the 22 of us who graduated on January 7, 1944, as second lieutenants. There were also three regular army infantry officers who had joined our class—Fred Parker, Charles Hunter, and Leon Turner—and they too received their wings.

After graduation, I enjoyed a 10-day leave in Washington, DC. I went to the city with Arthur Wilburn, who was in my class at Tuskegee and whose sister, Margo, I had met at graduation. During my 10 days in Washington, Margo and I developed quite a relationship. She was about five-foot-two, 110 pounds, with shoulder-length brown hair, green eyes, and a very smooth and fair complexion. My, my, my, such memories! In fact, I named the plane that I flew in combat "Margo." We exchanged letters while I was overseas, at least until I became a POW. I continued to write her but heard nothing more from her. When I returned to the States after the war, I discovered that some of my good buddies had taken care of Margo, and I never saw her again. It was during my time at Howard University and postwar visits that I developed many interesting friendships, including Margo, Gwen, Lil.

Alexander Jefferson and big-blue-eyed Lil at the Crystal Caverns nightclub in Washington, DC, 1944.

After my furlough in Washington, I returned to the Tuskegee Army Airfield for another several weeks to fly P-40s. These planes, with the angry tiger teeth emblazoned on their cowling, had returned from Burma and were really beat up. Nevertheless, it was a great thrill to hear the whine of that Allison engine and feel the torque of the prop on take off. Taxiing down the runway, you'd hear the popping and spitting of the engine because the magnetos didn't quite match the valve closings, and you'd get a lump in your throat because the nose sat so high you had to zigzag in order to see where you were going.

We did 10 hours in the P-40. Then, on February 5, 1944, we were transferred to Selfridge Army Air Base, 25 miles north of Detroit, for training in the P-39 Airacobra. We were assigned to the 553rd Replacement Squadron to be trained as replacement pilots for the 332nd Fighter Group, which had shipped overseas in early January.

The Airacobra was a sweet ship to fly because it flew so straight and level. Its liquid-cooled engine sat behind you, and it had a 37mm cannon that fired through the prop hub. That meant every time it fired, the recoil mechanism forced a decline in your airspeed of two or three miles per hour. The tricycle landing gear made it a very

Alexander Jefferson and Margo Wilburn at Crystal Caverns nightclub in Washington, DC, while on leave in 1944.

stable landing craft, which was a relief after the tail-dragging P-40. I got more than 100 hours in the Airacobra, and the only problem was avoiding any violent turns or stalls that might whip the plane over into a snap roll and an inverted, upside-down spin, which was usually fatal.

I especially enjoyed Selfridge because of its proximity to Paradise Valley, which was Detroit's black nightclub and entertainment district. It was located on the near east side of downtown Detroit in an area called "Black Bottom." In the 1930s and 1940s, because of rigidly proscribed racial segregation, almost all black businesses, entertainment spots, and available housing were crammed into its 66 square blocks. After Pearl Harbor, it became even more crowded with the arrival of thousands of Southern blacks who were hoping to find work in the defense plants. Living conditions were generally abysmal, with dilapidated, overcrowded housing and a definite shortage of indoor plumbing. There was also an abundance of gambling, prostitution, and gangsters. Without a doubt, you could find anything you wanted in the Valley—and a lot of things you didn't want.

Margo Wilburn.

Nevertheless, with its colorful people, world-class shows, black and tans, blind pigs, and showy elegance, it was a wonderful place to spend Friday and Saturday nights. Renowned jazz musicians such as Cab Calloway, Duke Ellington, and Louis Armstrong, along with local blues artists like John Lee Hooker, Big Maceo Merriweather, Bobo Jenkins, Calvin Frazier, and Boogie Woogie Red could be seen and heard in the Flame Show Bar, the Three Star Bar, the Forest Club, Sonny Wilson's Bar, and the Horseshoe Bar.

There were also beautiful young women to be found in the Valley, who certainly were not prostitutes, but who found a group of cocky young fighter pilots, full of vim, vigor, and vitality, to be quite attractive. Of course, my parents would not have approved of my escapades in the Valley, so I conducted myself appropriately. Even though I had a key to the front door of our Detroit home, I respected my father's unspoken rule, "Don't knock on my door after eleven o'clock." If I got home before that time, I had a bed. After eleven o'clock, I simply found a hotel room or some other convenient place to stay. My father was still working in the foundry, and went to bed at 11 p.m. in order to arise at 4 the next morning. He was still the physical and moral provider of the family, and as such it never occurred to me to challenge him.

Interestingly, when I returned to Detroit after the war, my first teaching job was located just six blocks north of the Valley. Although the nightlife was beginning to slow down by 1947, the outhouses remained; in fact, many of my students were still using them.

Night flying out of Selfridge was exciting, especially if you were flying in a tight circle, called a "luftberry," with four or five other P-39s around the Maccabees Building, in midtown Detroit: roaring 1,500-horsepower single engines, 11-foot props, flames shooting out of the open exhaust side stacks, kicking hard right rudder, throttles wide open in order to maintain altitude, which we figured to be about 200 feet, and speed, which was barely 150 mph! From there, we went streaming at treetop height over the Trowbridge and Harmon neighborhood, which was where the girls we were trying to impress lived. When we returned to base, we expected to catch hell and be reprimanded, but when interrogated, we, of course, were prepared to deny everything on a stack of Bibles.

Our instructors were First Lieutenants Charles Dryden and Spann Watson, along with another pilot whose name I cannot recall, who had all flown in combat in 1943 in North Africa with the all-black 99th Fighter Squadron. They were now assigned to our 553rd Fighter Replacement Squadron, along with the white instructors, to train replacement pilots for the 332nd Fighter and the 477th Bombardment Groups.

I'll never forget when Dryden, Watson, and this other black instructor plotted a low-level, cross-Michigan navigation flight to train us to fly on the deck, at treetop height, to avoid enemy fire. We first flew north to the Thumb area around Bad Axe, then west to Mt. Pleasant, south across Adrian and Monroe, and then back up the Detroit River to Lake St. Clair and Selfridge Field. Dryden told us, "There will be an instructor every 10 to 15 miles checking you out. We do not want to see anyone above 50 feet, and we mean no one!"

We had a ball. We dropped our planes down over the trees onto level fields and blew farmers off their tractors. The first plane through a farmyard blew chickens into the air, and the second and third plane would have chicken feathers and entrails clinging to their radiators. We had clothes lines wrapped around our props and grass stains on the tips. We played Follow the Leader coming up the Detroit River from Monroe. We were so low over the river that the 11-foot prop threw up a spray like a rooster tail. I don't know how many of us flew under the Ambassador Bridge, but I know I did. What fun!

Gunnery practice with our 37mm cannons on Lake Huron firing at a large 50-foot target floating on the water was tough. Every time you fired the cannon, you lost 5 to 7 mph of airspeed. Clarence "Red" Driver, trying to get too close to get a good score, was too low when he fired, and the shell hit the water and threw up a tall plume. His plane hit it, shuddered, and almost stalled, and the tail dragged the water before the prop pulled the plane out of the water. When he landed, the leading edge of the wing had been beaten back three to four inches where the water had hit it. The plane was "class 26" or "red-lined," which meant it was removed from flying status.

We stayed at Selfridge until May 10, 1944, when we were forced to leave because we attempted to integrate the officers' club in Luftberry Hall. Colonel Robert Selway, Jr. had been the commanding officer of the 332nd Fighter Group until it left Selfridge to go to Italy in January 1944, and he continued to command the 477th Bombard-ment Group, which remained at Selfridge. He was a West Point graduate who was determined to make life as miserable as possible for black airmen. He was convinced that African Americans were inferior and lacked the necessary skills to be combat pilots. He also believed they should never be put in supervisory positions. Agreeing with his racist policies were Lieutenant Colonel Charles A. Gayle, who was the com-manding officer of our 553rd Replacement Squadron; Colonel William L. Boyd, the base commander; and Major General Frank O'Driscoll Hunter of the 1st Air Force, all of whom were willing to jeopardize our training and the war effort in order to main-tain separate and second-class status for every African American under their com-mand. Their policies also violated Army Regulation 210-10, which mandated that officers' clubs and other social organizations offer "all officers on duty at the post the right to full membership, either permanent or temporary."

Matters came to a head when we raised grievances about being denied admittance to the officers' club in Luftberry Hall. The problem was all black officers were classi-fied on the morning report as "transient personnel," even though Dryden and Watson had been there for two months or longer. Upon arrival, all white officers were im-mediately classified as permanent, and only permanent personnel had officers' club privileges. To compound the indignity, we had to pay our monthly $6 officers' dues just like everybody else. When we complained to the club officer, who was, of course, white, he ordered the installation of a wooden bar in a tiny room in the barracks and told us that would be our Officers' Club. We refused to accept this, so every day we tried to enter the white Officers' Club, and every day we were turned away. The NAACP, the Urban League, and the *Michigan Chronicle* (a black newspaper) began pressuring the authorities to break down these barriers.

We were having gunnery practice over Lake Huron when our radios blared, "All officers report to the post theater, as you are, on the double!" That meant everyone, black and white, so we wheeled around, flew back to the base, and walked into the post theater still clad in our flying uniforms. There were 15 members of my Tuskegee class and approximately 25 or 30 other black officers on base who were ground and support personnel. I don't know how many white officers there were, but we all went inside trying to figure out what was going on. Someone yelled, "Ten-*hut!*" We popped to, and down the aisle came Major General Frank O'Driscoll Hunter, who had flown in for the meeting. Hunter then shouted, "At ease, gentlemen!" We sat down. He rambled on for about five or 10 minutes about problems at Selfridge, and then he said—and I remember his words exactly—"Gentlemen, this is my airfield. As long as I am in command, there will be no socialization between white and colored officers." He paused and then asked, "Are there any questions? If there are, I will deal with that man personally." Hell, we were second lieutenants, at the bottom of the officer ladder. What could we say? We sat there in shock and just looked at each other. Then somebody yelled, "Ten-*hut*!" and he walked out.

That was a Thursday. We were immediately confined to the post. The gates were locked, and our telephones were disconnected, so there was no way we could communicate with the outside world. In truth, we were under post arrest! On Saturday morning, a train backed into Selfridge, and all officers and enlisted personnel of the 553rd were loaded and locked in with just our bags. No one told us where we were going. We first went north to Port Huron, then across to Sarnia, Canada, and on to Niagara Falls, from where the train headed south. To this day, we have never seen the PCS (Permanent Change of Station) orders that sent us from Selfridge Army Air Base to Walterboro Army Airfield in South Carolina.

Although I didn't know the details at the time, the all-black 477th Bomber Group, which had likewise been preparing for combat, was also expelled from Selfridge. They were first sent to Godman Army Airfield, just outside of Fort Knox, Kentucky, and then, several months later, transferred to Freeman Army Airfield, Indiana, about 60 miles south of Indianapolis. They were still under the command of Colonel Selway, whose discriminatory policies once again led to trouble. On April 1, 1945, he posted an order restricting certain buildings to whites only. When several groups of black officers attempted to integrate the whites-only Officers' Club, he had them arrested. On April 9, Colonel Selway, with the approval of General Hunter, posted Regulation 85-2, which mandated the strict segregation of all base facilities. He then ordered all officers, black and white, to affirm and sign that they had read, understood, and accepted the conditions of Regulation 85-2. When 101 black officers, including future mayor of Detroit Coleman Young, who was one of the leaders, refused, the result was the so-called Freeman Field Mutiny. All were arrested. Some were court-martialed, and others received letters of reprimand. Army Chief of Staff General George C. Marshall and Chief of Air Staff General Barney Giles, fearing political repercussions, intervened and ordered the men released; however, not until 1995 were these men fully exonerated and their records expunged of all charges. In June, 1945, Colonel Selway was finally relieved of his command of the 477th Bombardment Group and replaced by Colonel Benjamin O. Davis, Jr., but by this time, it was too late for these men, and they never saw combat.

Walterboro Army Airfield was some 45 miles west of Charleston. It was one of a string of bases built along the Atlantic seaboard to defend against a possible invasion. It was another segregated base—and this time in a segregated state. When our train backed onto the base, we were greeted by white soldiers in full battle dress. There they stood, one every 30 feet along both sides of the train, with rifles and bayonets at the ready. We found out later they had been told to prepare for "a train full of rowdy niggers who have just rioted at Selfridge Field." There we were, in our Class A uniforms, trying to look our best. After we chatted with these soldiers about how things were in Walterboro, they quietly disappeared.

You have to understand that all this reflected the reality of the times. We were still second-class citizens, especially in the South. The unspoken rule in the military then was if you went counter to the local or state laws, no one would back you up. You were left on your own. We knew this. It was all part of coping, and we knew we had to deal with it. We tested the system, as best we could. It was a constant struggle, but our willingness to challenge the system helped us survive.

We were at Walterboro for only a few weeks, but again we tried to assert ourselves by integrating the post theater. There was a rope down the center of the theater to separate white and black soldiers. One night somebody cut the rope, after which the officer of the day closed the theater.

We were still flying the P-39 Airacobras at Walterboro when our old instructor from Selfridge, Charles Dryden, led three of us on an orientation and exploratory flight around the field and the surrounding countryside. I was on his right wing as Number Two; Robert Oneal was on his left at Number Three, with Frederick McIver next to him as Number Four. We flew over the swamps of South Carolina, the islands off the coast, and every little town within 25 or 30 miles. It was a Sunday morning, and, returning to base, Dryden proceeded to circle a Walterboro church at about 100 feet. We were separated from each other by maybe 20 feet. Then we flew right down the main street of Walterboro. It was great fun, and it allowed us to express our contempt for all the abuse and racism we had suffered. We fully expected to catch hell after landing, but, strangely enough, no one said anything, although the men in the tower certainly knew what we had done.

Another memory of Walterboro was wearing full jungle survival gear in case of engine failure on takeoff because there were all kinds of alligators and snakes in the swamp at the end of the runway.

On May 26, 1944, our group of 15 replacement pilots received orders to get on a train in Walterboro to travel to Camp Patrick Henry, Virginia, where we were going to board a ship for North Africa. We had these vouchers we were supposed to exchange in the tiny, 10×10-foot Walterboro Railroad Station for tickets that would entitle us to Pullman accommodations. The ticket clerk ordered us to go around to the back of the ticket office, but we refused, and things got nasty. We picked up our Thompson submachine guns, for which we were not supposed to have ammunition. Then a large group of angry white civilians armed with shotguns showed up, yelling and screaming that they were going to burn some niggers. We responded by ramming in our ammunition clips. All of a sudden, everything got very quiet. The train sat there for at least 45 minutes before the base colonel came screeching up in his staff car, accompanied by several trucks filled with white soldiers. The colonel tried to get us to give up our weapons, but we refused. Finally, the engineer said, "Get on board, fellas." We did, but we still didn't have our tickets.

I will never forget that train ride to Camp Patrick Henry because we were absolutely sure that when we arrived, we would be met by armed guards, arrested, and face court-martial. But nothing happened. We were assigned to barracks, along with our weapons, and settled in to await shipment overseas.

4 Combat

The 15 of us who graduated in Tuskegee Class 44-A were classified as replacement pilots for the 332nd Fighter Group. On June 3, 1944, we boarded a troopship bound for North Africa. Ironically, we black pilots were the only male officers who had our cabins above deck. There were thousands of enlisted personnel below deck, and their officers were with them. A contingency of 20 white nurses also had their cabins topside, right across the corridor from us. We visited, sunbathed, and ate together, and a good time was had by all.

The ship ran a solo, high-speed, zigzag course across the Atlantic. The captain said that we were doing up to 30 knots. Every 10 minutes or so, he would order the ship to change course about 15 degrees, I assume to make us a more difficult target for German submarines. After an uneventful and very pleasant seven days, we landed in Oran, on the northeast coast of Algeria, on June 8, 1944.

After just a few days in Oran, Algeria, the 15 of us, plus hundreds of regular troops, shipped out to Naples on an Indian tramp steamer. I have no idea why they put us on this Indian ship, but the smell and taste of the curry are still with me. The weather was balmy and sunny, which again made the voyage most enjoyable. When we docked in Naples, an army captain, who was in charge of the port battalion, loudly greeted us: "Hey, where in hell have you guys been? We've been waiting for you for a week." Instead of putting us in the regular barracks, he housed us in an apartment complex, most of whose residents were ladies of the evening.

We didn't realize that we were "distinguished" guests who were being watched by everyone up and down the echelon ladder. I'm not sure why; maybe it was because the 100th, 301st, and the 302nd Squadrons of the 332nd Fighter Group had been stationed at Capodichino Air Base, just outside of Naples, and black officers with wings always made white officers nervous. We stayed in Naples only three or four days, but we did have a wonderful time seeing the beautiful churches, buildings, parks, and Herculaneum, the city that Mount Vesuvius had covered but that had later been excavated. We hated to leave, but we had no choice.

The 15 of us climbed on 6 × 6 army trucks for a nightmare ride to the Ramitelli Air Base, which was located on the other side of the peninsula located on the heel of Italy about one-quarter of a mile from the Adriatic Sea. We drove on bumpy, two-lane, hazardous dirt roads for several hours before arriving at the shore of the Adriatic Sea early on the morning of June 20, 1944. Just as our trucks were pulling onto the base, we saw planes from the 332nd taking off on what would be their last P-47 combat mission. One of the planes pulled up into a steep climb, shuttered into a stall, fell off on a wing, and went in, erupting in a huge ball of flame. This was our introduction into the world of a combat pilot, but we were almost nonchalant about it because we were sure nothing like this could ever happen to any of us.

The airbase itself consisted of a metal strip runway that had been laid across a wheat field about one-quarter of a mile from the Adriatic. Next to the runway was a farmhouse that we used as group headquarters. Our 332nd Red Tail Fighter Group consisted of four squadrons and their designations: the 99th "Subsoil" had white trim tab colors on its rudders and ailerons, the 100th "Counter" black, the 301st "Bubbles" blue, and the 302nd "Doorknob" yellow.

The 52nd Fighter Group, flying P-51 Yellow Tails, was located about five miles north of us. The 325th Fighter Group's P-51 Checkertails were about 25 miles east of us along the coast at Lesina, Italy. And the 31st Fighter Squadron's P-51 Candy Stripe-Tails were located some 20 miles south of the 325th at San Severo, Italy. These last three were exclusively white squadrons.

Each squadron would put up four flights of four planes, plus two spares. The flights were always designated as Red, White, Blue, and Yellow. Spares were Squadron Spare One and Spare Two. The squadron's lead flight was Red One, and its pilot was the squadron leader for that mission. Red Two was his wingman and flew to his right and slightly behind him. Red Three was an element leader and flew to Red One's left and a little farther behind. Red Four flew on Red Three's left and a little behind him.

I was assigned to a tent in the 301st Squadron with William Faulkner, Othell Dickson, and Joseph Elsberry. Our tent, which had a wooden floor made from crates, was about 1,500 square feet, and because it was June, we were able to roll up the sides for much needed ventilation. We slept on cots covered with mosquito netting, but we also had DDT, in green-colored spray canisters, which really did a job on the mosquitoes. Our headquarters building was an Italian farmer's stucco block house. The runway was metal meshing, as were the parking ramps.

We arrived just in time for Ramitelli's transition from P-47s to P-51s. Getting accustomed to the P-51 was very easy. It was a smooth upgrade on the AT-6 and an absolutely outstanding airplane. We flew the B and C models. I flew my first mission after only three hours of transition, but I felt entirely assured and competent in spite of witnessing a fatal accident involving my tent mate, Othell Dickson. Dickson, who had graduated ahead of me in Class 43K, was a real hotshot, but he was flying the P-51 for the first time. From the flight line, I watched him fly across our tent area at about 50 feet, then pull up into a slow roll, fall out of it, barely recover, and come within 10 feet of hitting the ground. This brought all the guys out on the field, wondering who was this fool inviting a court-martial by the 332nd Fighter Group Commander, Colonel Benjamin O. Davis, Jr. Dickson then came back around again, and this time, starting at about 20 feet, he pulled up into a near 60-degree angle and simply fell out the maneuver. He went in upside-down just outside the tent area.

When we tried to recover his charred body, we found only the torso, minus head, feet, and hands, but still sitting in the pilot position and attitude. Dickson had not read the tech orders on the plane, or he would have known not to attempt any acrobatics with the fuselage gas tank holding more than half of its 85 gallon capacity. When it was too full, it put the center of gravity too far aft, resulting in loss of control when put in the wrong attitude. Again, my personal reaction was not so much emotional as it was practical. I said to myself, "RTDM!" (Read The Damn Manual!)

I have no detailed record of the missions I flew, but I know I flew 18 without ever missing a scheduled mission until I was shot down on August 12, 1944. We normally flew long-range missions, escorting B-24s and B-17s to their targets over Greece, Bulgaria, Hungary, Poland, Germany, and France, but we also flew strafing missions. I flew mostly as a wingman and did not have my own plane until just before my final mission. When new planes arrived or new engines were installed, the older pilots always had first choice. As a replacement pilot, I had to fly what was left. When I finally did get my own plane, I named her *Margo*, for the young lady I met while on leave in Washington, DC.

Our missions followed a prescribed routine. We'd awake by any means we could, trying not to disturb our tent mates in case they were not scheduled to fly and wanted

THE LUFTGANSTER — IN HIS HEYDAY!

Margo, *Alexander Jefferson's combat plane.*

to sleep. We'd wash, shave, brush our teeth, and then head for the mess tent, where we'd eat some very strange-tasting food that I suspect was flavored by the 100-octane gas that fueled the stoves. After this unsavory breakfast, we'd return to our tents, put on our flying suits, boots, gloves, chutes, goggles, and watches. The temperature at 30,000 feet was approximately –20 degrees, necessitating the heavy boots and gloves. An oxygen mask and tank were also necessary because of the lack of oxygen at that altitude. A well-dressed pursuit pilot would also wear a yellow Mae West (vest) and a dinghy, which were flotation devices if forced down over water. Once we were suited up, we'd grab our cigarettes and head to the group briefing tent. The briefing officer was usually Colonel Davis, the group commander, or his operations officer, Major Ed Gleed. A huge map of the entire European theater covered the wall. If a red string extended from Ramitelli and a green string from another airfield in Italy came together around the coast of Yugoslavia, we knew it would be an escort mission.

Someone would shout, "Attention!", and the briefing officer would enter. We would pop to and stand at attention. The briefing officer would respond, "At ease!", and everyone would sit down.

If the briefing officer said, "Gentlemen, today we go to Ploiesti," he would be greeted with a resounding "Oh, s***!" If there was only one red string ending in an area occupied by the enemy, it was a strafing mission, which usually also brought expletives from the fighter pilots because this meant being exposed to ground fire from enemy troops. If it was an escort mission, we would also be told whether we would be protecting B-17s or B-24s. We much preferred B-24s because the B-17s were slower, and we had to stay with them longer, which meant we used too much of our precious fuel.

The briefing officer would tell us the type of mission, the mission target, intelligence reports on anticipated ground fire and aerial attacks at the target, and possible partisan support, including what they might be wearing and their identifying armbands or headbands.

We would synchronize our watches and receive our engine startup and takeoff time, as well as our start-on course time, our estimated rendezvous time and place, and the estimated total mission time. An intelligence officer would then come in and give the latest flak report, informing us which areas to avoid because of heavy concentrations. These reports were invariably wrong, as we almost always encountered the most devastating flak over areas that intelligence had assured us were perfectly safe. In fact, for many World War II airmen, the term "military intelligence" still evokes laughter.

Later, in prison camp, with too much time on our hands, some unknown author wrote a tribute to military intelligence, which many of us who had been shot down read and appreciated:

Ode to S-2

S-2 is so amazing! They seem to have the knack,
Of knowing when, at what, is where—excepting fighters and flak!

S-2 is so ingenious! They seem to have the knack,
Of crediting all victories shot down by George—to Jack!

S-2 is so efficient! It seems it is their renown,
They get you quickly right to where you get yourself shot down!

S-2 is so unperturbed! They never flinch or frown,
They'll out fly any German ace, in any bar in town!

S-2 is so complex! They like to go on flings,
Before they leave for town each night, they borrow pilots' wings!

S-2 is so generous! They work for what they get,
To run the risk of map-osis or blonde or brunette!

S-2 is so valorous! They'd gladly take the air,
And fly all day for extra pay, in Flak Alley!

S-2 is so confident! They meet with great elation,
The enemy as he comes out, at the interrogation!

S-2 is so effective! They raise such commotion,
About our exploits in the air, that they get our promotions!

Many *Kriegies* appreciated this poem because it seemed that flak usually appeared precisely where S-2 indicated it would not appear! In addition, enemy fighters always seemed to appear and attack where S-2 insisted that it was impossible for them to do so! To add insult to injury, S-2 officers often showed up in the rest camps wearing wings and bragging to the girls about flying their heroic missions.

We would pile out of the briefing shack, get in Jeeps and trucks, and ride to our planes. In the meantime, our mechanics had been up most of the night preflighting our aircraft. We would walk around our planes and talk with the crew chiefs about any concerns. We'd then strap ourselves in, start the engines, check the dials, and clamp our feet on the brakes to prevent any premature movement of the 10,000-pound plane. For these missions, we had 92 gallons of gas inside each wing,

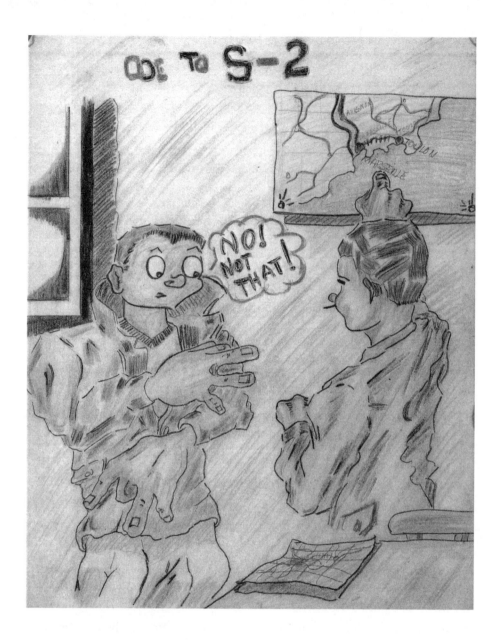

100 gallons hanging under each wing, and another 85 gallons in a tank behind the pilot. We also had two 50-caliber guns in each wing with 300 rounds for each gun.

We had only one runway from which all four squadrons would take off. Two squadrons would take off from each end. After the magneto engine check, the planes would sit idling until takeoff time. The lead plane would taxi onto the runway, waiting for the tower to fire off a green flare exactly at takeoff time. The Group Leader would then start rolling down the runway. Number Two would follow close behind. Number Three would move into place so he could follow. Fighting the turbulence of the preceding planes now became a challenge. This continued until 16 planes and the two spares had taken off. It was then that the lead plane of the second squadron would start his takeoff from the other end of the same runway.

While awaiting takeoff, with that big 11-foot prop spinning and those 1,500 horses pulling the plane, your pulse begins to race, especially when you look down the line and see the other 15 planes in your squadron slowly easing forward to begin taxiing down the ramp. Canopies are open, and the noise is deafening but exhilarating. You just hope the bastard behind you doesn't let up on his brakes and chew your tail off, or that the so-and-so on your left has his gun switch off or his finger off the trigger so he doesn't blow you to smithereens. You sit at the end of the runway and wait, your plane throbbing and threatening to bolt. Your legs are tied in knots from clamping your feet on the brakes. Fumes and dust penetrate your oxygen mask. There you sit, locked in, unable to move, worrying about somebody's prop chewing on your left, and your prop threatening the guy on your right. Finally, you look to your left and watch the 99th beginning to take off from the other end of the strip directly toward you. The first few guys pass over about 50 feet out in front of you. As Number Five and Six begin to hit the turbulence of the previous guys, they wobble back and forth. You look up, and a P-51 sails over your head with about 10 to 15 feet to spare!

After the 18 get off (16 plus two spares), it finally becomes our turn. Bubble Blue Leader wheels out, and we turn and taxi out to take off behind him. Throttle forward, engine pulling 60 inches of mercury, mixture rich, using left main tank, mags checked, dials in the green, prop pitch low, throttle pushed forward, forced back in seat by the tremendous acceleration, watching airspeed, easing off a bit, watching the torque, queuing in on the element leader, cutting him off, while he's cutting off the flight leader who is cutting off the squadron leader, who is cutting off the group

"Hitting the Blue."

leader: a giant luftberry in the sky, made up of 72 circling planes. The group circles the field twice before everyone is ready to get into tight formation: Four squadrons, 72 planes, off to pick up B-17s or B-24s.

Once in the air, the feeling was exhilarating! Sixty-four planes tooling and swirling, climbing and forming, joining up in groups of four, then into 12 and finally into 16, and then all four squadrons into a group of 64! But sitting on the ground, previous to takeoff, lined up at the end of the runway, waiting for permission of the 301st to take off was the only time that I felt completely and utterly scared—not frightened,

"Bringing Home a Cripple."

just plain scared—sitting at the end of the runway, 16 P-51s, wing tip to wing tip, loaded with 110-gallon tanks under each wing, 92 gallons inside each wing, 45 gallons in a tank behind you and four 50 caliber machine guns, each with more than 200 rounds, strapped in your seat with the engine idling while the 99th took off down the runway toward you. You fought the turbulence and prop wash of planes taking off over your head and the urge of your own plane to go forward, with your cramped legs stomping down on the brakes.

One of my most vivid memories of combat is sitting above those B-17s. It was always mind-boggling to look back as far as the eye could reach and see that 10- to 15-

"Combat Peel-Up."

mile string of bombers that might include as many as 1,000 planes. Up above, you'd see the contrails of our P-51s zigzagging back and forth over the straight contrails of the bombers. Typically, if the B-17s were flying at 24,000 feet, the 99th Squadron would be at 25,000 feet, the 100th at 26,000 feet, the 101st at 27,000 feet, and the 302nd at 28,000 feet. Because the bombers were so much slower, each fighter squadron would zigzag back and forth at 220 mph over the B-17s, which were flying at 160 mph. Occasionally, a squadron might be forced up to 32,000 feet, but in such thin air, one had to avoid sharp maneuvers, or the mushy controls might cause the plane to spin out.

"'A' Flight All Present."

So many things happen simultaneously: planes switching tanks, radios squawking, "Bogies (unknown planes) at three o'clock!" and then a loose, ragged formation automatically tightening when someone hollers, "Get the hell out of my ass!" Eyes get sharper, breathing becomes more rapid, heads weave right and left. Bubble Blue Leader comes in curt and sharp, "Bubble Blue, drop tanks on mark." Immediately, you switch your fuel from wing tanks to internal. Most of us had already done so when we first heard someone holler, "Bogie!" The sight of sixteen P-51s dropping tanks was spectacular: 32 silvery, bullet-shaped objects dropping like huge drops of rain, and often seeing the German planes turning away and refusing to come in.

Many escort missions were monotonous, five- or six-hour rides, but they could also be exhilarating. I remember on my fourth or fifth mission that our squadron got eight or nine kills. I didn't see a single one because I was too busy flying my element's wing, protecting his rear end. Above all, there was a great feeling of relief when all our planes returned safely to base.

My most unforgettable mission was flying cover over the Ploiesti oil fields. After we picked up our bombers at the border of Hungary and Romania, we encountered only sporadic anti-aircraft fire on the way to the target. Then, some 15 or 20 miles ahead, I saw a huge black cloud, shaped like a hockey puck, from 20,000 feet to about 26,000 feet. I could see a series of fires and lots of smoke rising from the ground underneath it, which appeared to be an oil refinery complex. The B-17s flew out on a 60-degree angle and then aimed directly for that black cloud. We pulled off to the left and orbited while they disappeared into the black cloud. Then, we saw four or five B-17s falling out of the bottom of the cloud, spinning down lazily, trailing smoke and flames. Unconsciously, I yelled, "Bail out, damn it! Get out of there!" Out of one of the planes I counted one, two, three chutes opening up. Then there was a big whoosh. The B-17 had exploded in a huge red ball of flames. Realism set in: Three chutes had opened; that meant seven men had died, right there in front of my eyes. Seven men no longer existed. I threw up into my oxygen mask—at 31,000 feet. That experience—including my crew chief's refusing to clean my oxygen mask after I returned to base—burned itself into my mind.

Many times on returning to home base, the 332nd would find stray bombers limping along after being shot up or hit by flak. We would pick them up and bring them home after their initial escort had deserted them. Often, they were returning from missions over the Ploiesti oil fields, and we would escort them to the Island of Vis off the Croatian coast. I had to land there twice myself because I was so low on fuel. The airfield was a literal boneyard. There were wrecked planes everywhere, mostly fighters and bombers that had barely made it back before crash landing. Both times when I was forced to land on Vis, my squadron had stayed with our bombers long past the allotted time. The fighter group that was supposed to rendezvous and relieve us had showed up late, which meant we didn't have enough fuel to make it home. "A" flight all present, depicted in my drawing, is when you flare out, side-slipping, fighting the slipstream of the guy about 20 feet to your left or right, five or six other guys on your

WHAT THE WELL DRESSED PURSUIT PILOT
WEARS ON A MISSION.

MAE WEST
OXYGEN MASK
MIKE IN MASK

KAAKI UNIFORM
HEAVY LEATHER GLOVES
FUR-LINED BOOTS

HELMET ; GOGGLES
HEAD-SET
PARACHUTE
RUBBER SEAT PAD
BACK DINGY

tail, low on fuel just like you. You can't go around, and they're eating up your tail. Each man turns off the runway at the first possible turn-off, with power on to the end of the runway.

What the well-dressed pursuit pilot wears . . . The temperature at 30,000 feet was approximately –20 degrees, necessitating the heavy boots and gloves. The oxygen mask and tank were necessary because of the lack of oxygen at that altitude. The yellow Mae West (vest) and the dinghy were flotation devices if forced down over water.

I remember sitting on the wing of my plane in Vis surveying all the wrecked airplanes while the ground crew gassed me up. I also remember drinking a wretched

"What the well-dressed pursuit pilot wears . . ."

cup of coffee, my first of the day, because we never drank coffee in the morning before a long mission that could last up to six hours. We did have a small relief tube in the plane, but you couldn't get to your personal equipment through the parachute straps and your flying suit.

After every mission, we were debriefed. Intelligence was always interested in determining whether what they had told us in the morning was helpful. Of course, what we actually experienced was almost always the opposite of what they had told us to expect.

I don't remember much else about camp life at Ramitelli, except that I still made my model airplanes. Even in wartime, my life settled into some kind of routine, at least until I was shot down and captured on August 12, 1944.

5 Captured!

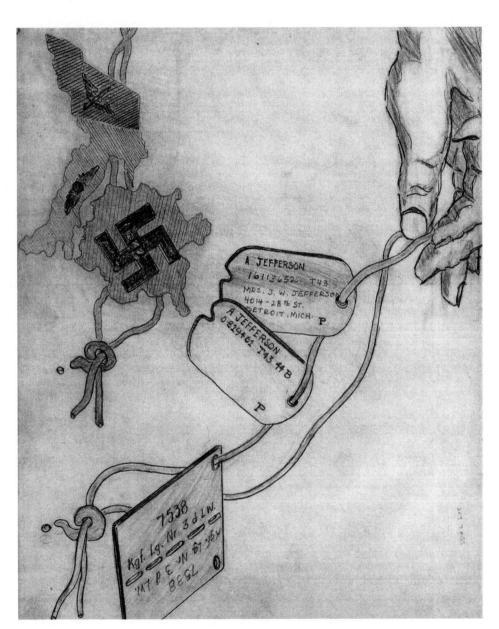

Hand and dog tags.

If the war had not come along, I would have been a graduate of Howard University and probably working for the U.S. Post Office because at the time, that was the only future for a black male, except perhaps becoming a preacher, lawyer, or doctor. The hand and dog tags depicted in my drawing represent the many strands of my life in 1944. The first dog tag under the hand, which represents a cadet, was for my training in Alabama. The next down, the tag of an officer, was for my combat flying over Italy. The bottom tag, which can be broken in half to make two, was for becoming a German POW. The dangling question mark suggested my uncertain future.

On August 12, 1944, I was a pilot with the 301st Fighter Squadron, 332nd Fighter Group, 15th Air Force. I was flying my nineteenth mission, which was to strafe and knock out radar stations at Toulon Harbor on the southern coast of France to prevent the Germans from detecting the Allied invasion ships, which three days later, as part of Operation Dragoon, would land between Marseilles and Nice.

What follows here is the factual account of what happened the day I was shot down, written one month after it occurred, because I realized that if I waited until much later, some of the minute details of that fateful day might be forgotten or possibly twisted.

It was a beautiful clear day, with unlimited visibility, when our 16 P-51s flew in over the coast in four flights of four each. The first three sets of four went in, hit the target at low level, and flew out to sea. We were the last flight. As we dived in from 15,000 feet at about 400 knots, I was Tail-End Charlie, which meant I was the last plane to go in. When our squadron leader called for us to drop our 100-gallon tanks, somehow my tanks got hung up, and I was slow dropping them. In order to catch up, I had to push everything to the wall, with my airspeed almost redlined. I was pulling about 60 inches of manifold pressure, the plane was shaking and rocking, but I did get back into position just before our flight began to fire on the target.

Halfway down, I could see blinking red lights over the target; in fact, the entire side of the cliff in front of the radar towers was covered with anti-aircraft fire. About 1,000 yards from the target, out of the corner of my eye, I saw Bob Daniels's Number Two plane take two direct hits. He began trailing black smoke and headed out to sea. I found out later he had elected to set down on the water, which was not advised, because the air scoop could pull the plane under water before the pilot could extricate himself. Nevertheless, Daniels got out and floated on the water until the Germans picked him up.

*Going in for the kill at
Toulon Harbor.*

*Looking out my cockpit and seeing
Bob Daniels' plane hit.*

By this time, we were down to 300 feet, flying at more than 400 mph. Looking ahead, I could see the first flight of four getting hits on the towers and veering out to sea. Right behind them came the second and third flights, which also got their hits and banked out to sea. Then we came into position. With the target in range, my ship was bucking and shaking. Anti-aircraft fire was coming up on all sides. My oil pressure and coolant temp needles were in the red, with everything else at the top of the green, about to go red.

As I passed over the target at about 50 feet, I felt a loud thump shake the plane. I glanced at the instrument panel, and now everything was in the red. I felt a tremendous rush of air. I looked up, and there was a hole in the top of my canopy just in front of my head. I thought, "What the hell?!" Fire and smoke were filling the cockpit. I looked down and saw that flames were coming up through a hole in the floor between my feet and scorching my gloves and boots. I pulled up into a loop to get some altitude, jerked the red knob on the instrument panel, and popped the canopy. At the same time, I racked in the forward trim tab on the elevator with my left hand. At the top of the loop, I punched the safety belt release and let go of the stick. The forward trim tab was supposed to pitch the nose down, but because the plane was upside down, the nose went up abruptly, and I was thrown out. I figure I got out at about 800 feet.

I can still see the tail, including the rivets, as it went whizzing by. During the nine months of training, due to the war, we never had a minute on how to bail out of a plane. I looked down and saw the trees. I pulled the D-ring. I looked at it in my hand and thought, "Some SOB sold the silk." The rumor back at the base was that someone had been stealing the silk out of the parachutes and selling it to the Italians. So when my chute did not immediately open, I thought that had happened to me. But just then the chute popped, and all I could see was green. I fell through some trees and hit squarely on my feet and rolled over. I sustained cuts and bruises on my arms and legs. Fortunately, I was wearing paratrooper jump boots, which gave extra support to my ankles.

At the time, things are happening so fast you don't have time to get scared. It's only a couple of days later, when you have time to think about what happened, that it all hits you. Intelligence had told us French resistance fighters were in the area, so we were supposed to dig a hole, hide our parachute, and wait for the French to find us.

A rough landing.

Hell, I hit the ground, rolled over, and looked up into the muzzle of a Mauser and a German soldier saying, *"Ja, ja, Herr Leutnant. Für sie ist der Krieg vorbei."* ("Ah, yes, Lieutenant. For you, the war is over.") I had landed right in the middle of the 20mm gun crew that had shot me down.

The other guys in my flight looked back and saw my plane go in, but they didn't see me get out. They thought I "bought the farm" and reported me killed in action (KIA). My mother and dad subsequently received the dreaded KIA telegram. Not until several weeks later did the International Red Cross notify them that I was a prisoner of war.

The first things my captors took were my cigarettes, my Parker pen, and my wrist-watch. They then transported me in a car several miles east of Toulon to a small villa overlooking the Mediterranean. A German officer was seated at a glass table on the veranda. I saluted because he had rank on his shoulders. In perfect English, he said, "Have a seat, lieutenant, and thanks for the Lucky Strikes!" He spoke very formally and asked me how things were in the States. I replied, as S-2 had instructed us, with name, rank, and serial number. He ignored this and asked whether I had ever been in Atlanta. I told him I hadn't, although, of course, I had spent four years attending Clark College. He talked about the black clubs on Auburn Avenue and the good times he had enjoyed in the various bars and hotels. He then asked whether I had ever been in Washington, DC. I again told him no, even though I had attended Howard University.

He then proceeded to tell me about his days at the University of Michigan, naming streets, fraternity houses, and restaurants. It turned out he had graduated from the University of Michigan in 1936, with a PhD in political science. After returning to Germany, he was called into the army and eventually assigned to the anti-aircraft unit that shot me down. He was a jazz fan and talked about the Howard Theater and the Crystal Caverns nightclub in Washington, where all the black jazz artists appeared, and then he started talking about Detroit's Paradise Valley. His whole demeanor changed, and he became much friendlier. He told me about boarding the Oakland streetcar next to the library behind the J. L. Hudson Department Store in downtown Detroit, and how it proceeded east on Adams, past the "colored" YMCA and the Three Sixes Nightclub and then turned north on Hastings and then west on Forest Street, where Sonny Wilson's Bar was on the corner. He even named the bartenders and the girls across the street in the "hotel." For the next 30 minutes or so, I sat listening while he smoked my Lucky Strikes and excitedly told me about his Detroit experiences, especially about all the fun he had while drinking and carousing with the local girls. He finally said to me, "Some of the best times in my life were spent in the Valley. Let's hope this war ends soon so we can get back to the things that really matter." With that he offered me one of my cigarettes, shook my hand, then stood on the porch in a typical Nazi stance, watching silently and forlornly as they loaded me aboard a truck to be transported to a POW camp in Germany. I thought to myself, it really is a small world. At first, he had rubbed my feelings a little raw, hearing him speak about the "good" loving he received from our black girls back home. In the end, however, I was truly thankful for their efforts on behalf of the war. Truly thankful, indeed.

I have no idea what happened to him, but after I left, I was taken to a Luftwaffe field about 20 miles north of Toulon and locked in a barracks room overnight. The next day, the Germans brought in Bob Daniels, whom they had picked up in the Mediterranean. Very early the next morning, which was August 14, the two of us, with two guards, departed for Marseilles by bus where we boarded a train and headed up the Rhone Valley to Orange. We rode on a flatbed car along with at least 20 88mm anti-aircraft guns, the artillery responsible for the terrific flak that our bombers had to endure over Germany. Fortunately, no Allied planes spotted us. From Orange, we got rides on wagons and trucks, and also did some walking before we reached Valence, where we stayed overnight in a barn that reeked of cows and sheep. While we were groping around the barn in the dark, we came across Richard Macon from the 302nd Squadron, who had been shot down on the same mission near Montpellier, about 40 miles down the coast from Toulon. He was in bad shape and appeared to have a fractured neck because every time he moved abruptly, he passed out. We braced his neck and head to make them immovable. When we got him up the next morning, he had to walk very slowly, trying not to move his head.

The next day, the three of us continued up the Rhone Valley toward Lyon in the back of a truck with our two guards. Naturally, we were a little concerned. We had heard that the Germans considered blacks to be apes and all kinds of other stereotypes. We knew what they thought about Jews. We had encountered some racism in Italy, although we later found out that was mostly due to white American soldiers telling the Italians terrible things about us. But our two regular army Wehrmacht guards saw us as officers, even celebrities, and treated us accordingly. They even shared their food with us, which consisted of grapes, melons, hard brown bread, margarine, and blood sausage they had bartered for with French civilians. Blood sausage is made from congealed animal blood, but I learned to relish it.

On August 20, we reached Oberursel, Germany, just outside of Frankfurt, but we only stayed there for a couple of days before we were moved some 30 miles north to

Alexander Jefferson's POW identification card.

Dulag Luft just northwest of Wetzlar, which was the central interrogation center for captured airmen. Dulag Luft stands for *Durchgangslager der Luftwaffe* (air force transit camp). I was thoroughly searched, photographed, fingerprinted, and given POW number 7538. The photo depicts a tired, unshaven, dirty face that shows the results of what I had endured since my capture. In fact, I do look a bit like a *Luftgangster*—an "air gangster," as the Germans called Allied fliers.

During the four days I spent in Dulag Luft, I was kept in solitary confinement, although allowed my first shower, shave, sleep, and hot meal since being captured. This meal consisted of oatmeal, German bread, cocoa, and powdered eggs, some of which obviously came from a Red Cross parcel. It tasted good, especially because all I had eaten since my capture on the twelfth was the food our guards shared with us traveling up the Rhone.

Jefferson's Tuskegee graduating class, January 7, 1944.

During my third day in Dulag Luft, I was taken to an office to be interrogated. When I entered the room, I faced a German officer sitting behind a desk staring at me. In perfect English, but a bit too cordially, he said, "Have a seat, lieutenant." I sat down across the desk from him and noticed that he was thumbing through a large notebook, the cover of which stated, *332nd Fighter Group—Negroes—Red Tails*. Without saying a word, he slowly flipped through pages. I immediately recognized the photographs of several of the Tuskegee classes that had graduated before mine. Suddenly, he stopped and said, "Lieutenant, isn't this you?" He was pointing to my January 7, 1944, graduation class picture, taken at Tuskegee Army Airfield, and there I was, standing fifth from the right in the top row.

He proceeded to tell me my life story, and he seemed to know more about me than I knew about myself. He told me my father's Social Security number, his take-home pay, the taxes he paid on his home, all my grades at Clark College and Howard University, and even my sister's college grades. He told me about our mission over southern France, and, even more amazingly, he had my crew chief's 10-hour inspection on the plane I flew, which was completed the day before I was shot down. Some of this information was public record, but not the inspection or our mission. The Germans had to have had somebody at Ramitelli Air Base or higher up the line who was giving them information.

While he was telling me all this, I sat and smoked his cigarettes. Interestingly, he asked me no questions about tactics, targets, or equipment. He was very condescending and acted as though Germany respected blacks. But, if Germany had still been winning the war, I am quite sure it would have been very much different for me and the other black prisoners. I would guess they would have treated us in much the same manner they treated the Jews because they considered us both to be less than human. I later learned that the man questioning me was Hans Scharf, Germany's most infamous and successful World War II interrogator of POWs.

Shortly after being interrogated, the three of us left Dulag Luft for the final leg of our journey to our permanent POW camp at Stalag Luft III, which was located just outside the town of Sagan, close to what was then Germany's eastern border. By the time we reached Sagan on August 26, we had been underway for two weeks and had traveled, by a wide variety of means, from southern France all the way across Germany, a distance of several hundred miles.

One way ticket to Das Reich: Alexander Jefferson's travels as a German POW.

6 Stalag Luft III

This drawing, which was originally done by another pilot, circulated around Stalag Luft III. Each of us made alterations. I added the service cap and the bars on the collar.

Of course, this was a caricature, as every man in the camp was honored to have been able to fly and get his wings. Flying had been an ongoing fascination with me my entire life. I clearly remembered Lindbergh's flight across the Atlantic, the Great Zeppelin flying over Detroit, and the whole phenomenon of flight during the late 1930s and early 1940s. I read every comic book and magazine that had anything to do with flight and constructed all kinds of model airplanes. I even drew the plans and built a model of a super English float plane with a 49-inch wing span. The actual plane had held the world speed record in 1933. I was so fascinated by planes that I even skipped grade school class to go out to a small airport, where I washed planes and did other odd jobs for rides.

I tried to look on my captivity as just one among many extraordinary experiences. The only time I really became frightened was during the three-day train ride from Dulag Luft to Stalag Luft III. Daniels, Macon, and I were again escorted by two German guards with rifles. When the train stopped in a small town, and we walked through the station to catch another train, we were accosted by a group of Hitler Youth. They were singing some kind of marching song, but when they spotted us, they began yelling obscenities and haranguing us. They called us *Luftgangster* (air gangsters) and *Terrorflieger* (pilots of terror) and all kinds of other things, which, fortunately, I did not understand. Scared? You're damn right I was scared. We had heard of downed Allied flying personnel being beaten and even murdered by angry German civilians. After all, what would American citizens have done to German airmen who had just bombed their homes and cities?

Our two guards were all but overwhelmed before they managed to get us through the station and onto the waiting train where they locked us in our compartment. These crazy youngsters were still running up and down the train platform, screaming and yelling at the top of their lungs. By this time, some of the nearby civilians had also become aroused. We fully expected to be dragged off the train and killed. Our guards even had to threaten to shoot at the mob before the train finally pulled out of the station. It's funny, but I was never really frightened when I was shot down or during my eight and a half months in captivity, but in that damn train station, I was scared to death!

When we arrived at Stalag Luft III on August 26, 1944, Richard Macon was immediately sent to the camp hospital, and Robert Daniels was assigned to a room in another barracks. After they left, I had quite a surprise. The camp was already overcrowded, so each barracks room had to choose a new roommate.

Approximately 200 of us new POWs were lined up, and a representative from each room walked down the line and picked out a new roommate. A dyed-in-the-wool cracker with the deepest Southern drawl imaginable walked up to me and said, "Ah think I'll take this boy." I was naturally very apprehensive, thinking that I had not come all the way from the USA to be with a bunch of rednecks. I really wanted to reject what I was sure would simply result in discrimination and humiliation. However, standing immediately behind this good ole boy was an American full bird colonel. He motioned and said, "Lieutenant, you go with him." I saluted and went off to my assigned room. What I found was a real hodgepodge of ethnicities: two or three Southerners, a Jew, a couple of guys from Brooklyn, a couple more from God knows where, and Hal Erickson from Detroit. I was the only black.

I soon discovered why they had chosen me. Their room happened to house escape materials, and they wanted to make sure they didn't get a German plant or an American turncoat. They later told me, "We knew we could trust you." I thought it then and have said it many times since, "Ain't that a bitch!" At home, black soldiers caught hell from SOBs just like the guy who had selected me. Now, 5,000 miles from home, they can trust a black man because they are scared to death of a strange white face. Ain't that a bitch!

Stalag Luft III was a huge prison camp located near Sagan, a town of some 25,000 inhabitants, located about 90 miles southeast of Berlin on the Bóbr River, which itself was a tributary of the Oder. Today, the town belongs to Poland. When Luft III opened in April 1942, it housed primarily British airmen and Commonwealth prisoners, but by the time I arrived on August 26, 1944, the majority of Stalag Luft III prisoners were American airmen.

The comparatively principled Luftwaffe administered Stalag Luft III. I know of no brutal treatment of American or English officers, with the exception of the SS's execution of the 50 English officers who were captured after they escaped through a tunnel in "The Great Escape," as it was called in at least two books and one very successful Hollywood film.

Stalag Luft III was a dirty brown maze of wooden huts, guard towers, and barbed wire hacked out of the pine forests near the town of Sagan, about 100 miles southeast of Berlin. The German Luftwaffe had opened the camp in April, 1942. By January, 1945, it had become a city larger than Sagan, with a population of more than 11,000 officer POWs. It was surrounded by two barbed-wire fences: one 10 feet high, and the other 3 feet in height. The guard towers, called "goon boxes," were always in view and

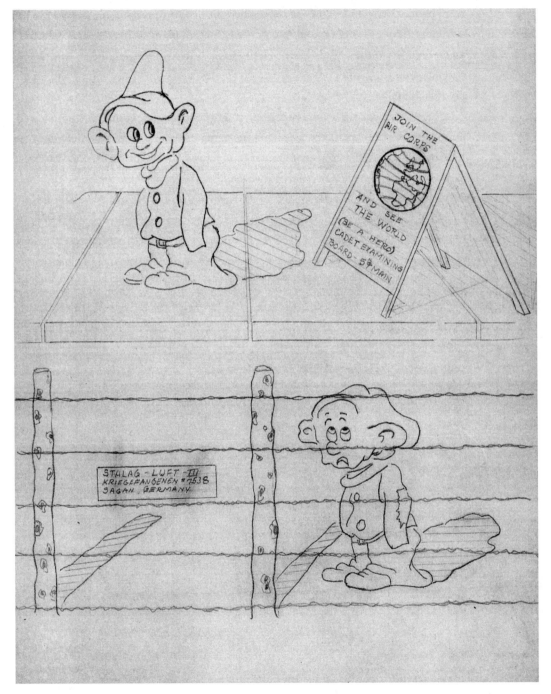

were manned day and night. At night, the omnipresent searchlight was always on, sweeping across the compound. Many rooms put up blankets over their windows in an attempt to cut the nightly glare of light. In addition to the searchlights, the guards had machine guns, rifles, telephones, field glasses, and even a seismograph to record possible tunneling activities.

When I arrived, the camp consisted of only the North, South, and West compounds. When we eventually evacuated the camp on January 29, 1945, it had grown to a sprawling complex of six compounds and more than 10,000 prisoners. The entire camp was surrounded by two barbed-wire fences. The space between these two fences was considered no-man's land, and any prisoner could be shot if he entered this space. Thirty feet inside the 10-foot fence was a guard rail. This was the perimeter that prisoners would walk—"pounding the perimeter"—thrashing out beefs, gripes, philosophy, and likes and dislikes. This is where Frank Haddick and I formed a lasting friendship. We walked many a mile around that six-tenth–mile boundary.

This little gem of a song was something we learned from the British, You can imagine the gusto and bravado with which we Americans raised our lusty voices when the Germans came within ear shot!

Remember?
Here we are at Stalag Luft 3,
Drinking beer at the bar,
With lovely girls to buy us beer,
Like bloody hell we are!
We traveled here in Luxury,
The whole trip for a Quid,
A sleeping berth for each of us,
Like bloody hell we did!
Our feather beds are two feet deep.
Our carpets always new.
In easy chairs, we spend the day.
Like bloody hell we would!
The "Goons" are really "wizard chaps,"
Their hopes of victory good.
We'd change them places any day,
Like bloody hell we will!
When winter comes and snows aground,

The temperatures at nil,
We'll find hot water bottles in our beds.
Like bloody hell we will!
It's heaven on earth at Stalag Luft 3,
A life we'd hate to miss,
It's everything we'd hate to miss,
Like bloody hell it is!
And when this war is over,
And Jerry gets his fill,
We'll remember all that's happened here,
My bloody oath we will!

Layout of compounds in Stalag Luft III.

South Compound, Stalag Luft III

Der Abort (latrine, meant to accommodate 30 men)
Cookhouse (administrative offices in north end; large boilers in center for heating soup and hot water)
Wash House (cold water)
Hot Shower Building
Theater (also contained classrooms and library)
Block 128, Jefferson's "home"

Block 128's coat of arms: "Semper Excreta"— translation, "Always in the shit."

The cell. Note the names on the bunks—Harold E. Erickson and Louis Gill. Both were residents of Livonia, Michigan, a suburb of Detroit. Gill and I attended the weekly POW sessions at the Veterans' Hospital.

Room 8, Block 128

Jefferson sketches his bunkmates from his top-bunk vantage.

Wash Day.

Two men knitting.

I was housed in Room 8, Block 128, which was our barracks building in South Compound. The room itself was 16 × 16 feet, with two triple bunks and two double bunks. And, in spite of my initial reservations, my roommates turned out to be extremely open-minded. Of course, with our varied backgrounds, we did have lots of interesting discussions concerning race and discrimination, but we all came to respect one another. I even drew a coat of arms for our guys. Of course, we tried not to take things too seriously, as you can tell by the "Fickle Finger of Fate" located at the top of our shield and our motto, "Semper in Excretia." "KLIM" (upper left-hand corner of the Coat of Arms) was *milk* spelled backward. This powdered milk was basic to all the puddings, cakes, and various other dishes we *Kriegies* prepared. The Player cigarettes in the lower right of the shield were British. They were foul smelling and almost impossible to smoke. When bartering and negotiating, seven of them were worth one American cigarette. Even the Germans didn't like them, and the Polish peasants would never barter for them if they could barter for American cigarettes. The wings at the bottom left represent pilot, bombardier, and navigator. The roster of Room 8, Block 128 is listed at the lower right. Ironically, 2nd Lt. Harold E. Erickson was from Livonia, Michigan, approximately 15 miles away from my home, but we never knew this until approximately ten years ago. What a happy reunion!

You can also tell by some of my room drawings that we weren't the best of housekeepers. Room 8, Block 128 was the room in which I spent six months. When I arrived in Stalag Luft III, I was issued a cup, two blankets, a mattress cover, two sheets, and a pillow. Each room in the barracks already held eight men, and the double bunks were already full. We then had to substitute two double bunks for a triple bunk to accommodate two additional men. Because Donley and I were the last two men assigned to the room, we inherited the two top bunks. Donley's *Kriegie* number was very close to mine; his was 7511, mine was 7538.

The one-and-one-half foot square, three foot–high stove offered the only heat in the room, which was inadequately heated by coal secured from the Germans and wood that we *Kriegies* got from the stumps we pulled.

The temperature in the room never reached 70 degrees Fahrenheit during December and January. A toaster sat on top of the stove. I can still sense, feel, and smell the stench of toasted Limburger cheese. But it did taste good indeed! A coal bin was immediately in back of the porcelain-covered stove. Each man had a cup that was lined up under the shelf that held that dense, black German bread that had the consistency of sawdust. Cooking utensils were stacked under the table on which food was prepared. The can at the door held rolls of paper with which to light the fire in the stove. Each room had a single 60-watt bulb hanging from the ceiling, which was our only illumination. Notice that Erickson's POW number is quite low, which means that he had been in the camp at least a year or more. Donley had a high number, which meant he was a new arrival. The Germans required that the names and POW numbers be printed on the side of the beds.

Clearly, the only privacy that a POW had was his bunk. A small shelf held his toilet articles, and his coat and jackets hung on the head of the bed. His drying clothes were strung across the room. Above the cabinet next to the door were the boxes in which the Red Cross food parcels arrived, which we then used for storage. I was the last guy to come into this room; therefore, my bunk was the top of the second triple bunk, which meant it was the warmest in winter! The mattresses were cotton or muslin, filled with straw and laid on eight cross boards. For the construction of the tunnels, each man had to contribute boards, which were used to shore up the tunnel walls. By January, we were sleeping on four boards! And the Germans in their barracks checks and searches never became aware of the disappearance of those boards or what they were being used for.

Kriegies spent much of their time knitting and sewing sweaters, gloves, socks, scarves, and other apparel in preparation for a winter that was one of the coldest on record for this part of Europe. Unfortunately, the windows were very inefficient and leaked cold air like a sieve.

We had a nearby washhouse, where we did most of our washing in cold water in tin basins. We occasionally got to take a shower in a different building. We had soap in our Red Cross parcels, so we were able to keep ourselves relatively clean, which was very important because body lice were everywhere, as well as various other creepy and crawling vermin. Of course, military discipline also helped inspire us to keep ourselves clean.

I drew lots of pictures to keep from being bored. The Red Cross supplied us with paper, pencils, pens, and ink. They also sent us all kinds of games, as well as a wide variety of sporting equipment so we could play baseball, basketball, and even soccer. I played lots of cards, and I spent a lot of time reading. Despite many planned

The washroom.

activities, the men were often lonely and frustrated. To relieve the boredom, they built a theater, a church, and an ice rink, and created a concert and dance band. However, the most impressive creation was the library we put together in Stalag Luft III. Friends and families sent us books, as did the Red Cross. We had books on philosophy, psychology, theater, government, sociology, and lots of fiction, including bestsellers. I must have read 50 or 60 books during my five months in Stalag Luft III. A partial list included *The Robe*; *Kings Row*; *Lost Horizon*; *Brave New World*; *For Whom the Bell Tolls*; *The Moon and Sixpence*; *Of Human Bondage*; *The Razor's Edge*; *The Fountainhead*; *Northwest Passage*; *Look Homeward, Angel*; *Nana*; *A Farewell to Arms*; *Life in a Putty Knife Factory*; *Pride and Prejudice*; *The Case for Germany*; *The Gioconda Smile*; *This Above All*; *Random Harvest*; *How Odd of God*; *Candide*; *Jews Must Live*; *Oliver Wiswell*; *Captain Caution*; and even *Mein Kampf*.

Each room had a work roster that rotated from man to man. The daily "stooge" did all the work duties, such as sweeping the room, cooking, peeling potatoes, making

Our library.

REFERENCE LIBRARY — IN BLOCK 133

the fire, carrying out the ashes, and getting the water for cooking in the vessel labeled *Kein Trinkvasser.*

The Germans broadcast their version of the news two or three times a day from a speaker on the cookhouse wall. The POWs, however, displayed their inventiveness in other, more creative ways. We received updates on the war's progress from newly arriving prisoners and from clandestine radios daily from the BBC (British Broadcasting Company) broadcasts. Some of us had illegal radio sets that were smuggled in or built from materials obtained by bribing the guards. At a certain time of the day or night, there was a broadcast from London with news. We knew about the progress of the war before the Germans could post it on the bulletin boards or admit to many of their defeats. The news would be sent around by a newsman who would go room to room.

Many of the *Kriegies* spent much of their time walking around the perimeter. They walked around this path as a means of relieving boredom and fatigue, and as a way of discussing matters with other *Kriegies.* Life was such drudgery. Many men suffered moods of depression from a lack of mail. Others occupied their time in drawing, reading, and knitting. Still others participated in musical, dramatic, or choral groups. Summer sports included baseball, football, and table tennis, with equipment supplied by the Red Cross and YMCA.

There were 12 of us Tuskegee Airmen in Luft III. I was in the South Compound with Woody Morgan, Robert Daniels, and Richard Macon, after he got out of the hospital. Scotty Halfcock and Lewis Smith were in the West Compound. The other six were in either Center or North Compound. The North Compound held primarily British prisoners.

Surprisingly, there were few fighter pilots in Stalag Luft III. Most American prisoners had flown bombers. Of course, as Tuskegee Airmen, we were held in high esteem. We were also a bit older and more mature. All of us were college graduates although some of the white pilots were not.

Did I experience any overt racism or general resentment on the part of the white POWs? Understandably, I felt an undercurrent of hesitancy and a kind of guarded inquisitiveness. Some of these men had been prisoners for more than two years and had no idea that blacks were now pilots and officers in the Army Air Corps. This was very strange to them, but then one day, a B-17 crewmember arrived in Stalag Luft III. When he spotted me, he ran over, grabbed and hugged me, and exclaimed,

"You're a Red Tail! You goddamn Red Tails are the best damned unit! If the Red Tails had been with us, we'd have made it back home! You guys saved our asses so many times!" After that encounter, the reputation of the 332nd Fighter Group spread quickly throughout the camp.

The camp was very well organized. After all, we were still in the military. The senior officer for the Americans was Colonel Charles G. Goodrich, and he enforced military discipline straight down the line. Each morning and evening, all POWs had to fall out for *Appell* (roll call). Colonel Goodrich would form us into blocks on the parade ground. *Appell* usually took about 30 minutes, unless the count was off, which meant each of us would be scrutinized to make sure we matched the photo on our German ID card. This could take two or three hours, which was not all that pleasant in freezing weather.

The Geneva Convention mandated that officers were not to work. Nevertheless, we would occasionally volunteer to do something that would help make life easier for us. For example, the land on which Stalag Luft III was constructed had been a pine forest with sandy soil, and there were still lots of stumps, especially near the athletic field where we were allowed to play baseball and various other games. We wanted them out, so we constructed a Rube Goldberg contraption that allowed us to get enough leverage to pull out the stumps. I was far too small to be of much help, but I did sketch the whole affair.

The stumps were left between the two-foot, no-touch fence and the 10-foot double barbed-wire fence. The stump puller worked on the principle of leverage and was very powerful. Quite naturally, each job had to have a sidewalk superintendent. And since my weight was barely 110 pounds dripping wet, that job fell to me! A heavy man on the end of the lever exerted more energy, and thus more leverage and power to pull up the stump. These stumps were then used for heating and cooking. Each room had a turn using the stump puller, and this was the only time we were allowed between the forbidden wire and the barbed-wire fence.

In the beginning, we all dreamed of wine, women, song, and food. After the first week, we forgot about the wine; next we forgot about the song. After four or five more weeks, we forgot about the women—but we never forget about food.

When you mix sugar and raisins with potatoes and water, what do you get? Well, *Kriegies* were very inventive to say the least. They even threw in some rice, prunes,

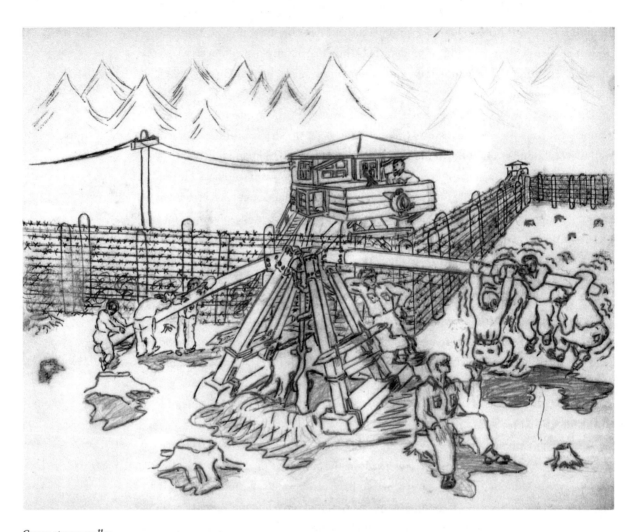

Camp stump puller.

and German-issued honey. Given our state of malnutrition and physical deterioration, the effects were predictably horrendous.

Each barracks had a stove to serve 120 men. Each room was assigned a time each day to use the stove for baking or the general preparation of meals. We also had a small stove in our room we could use when some kind of fuel was available.

We augmented our German rations with our Red Cross parcels, which arrived more or less on a regular basis although not after we were moved to Stalag VIIA in Moosburg. These were lifesavers, but the guys still dreamed of some good old home cooking.

The importance of Red Cross food parcels cannot be overstated. The meager rations supplied by our captors were supplemented by the Red Cross food parcels, which added 1,000 calories to a prisoner's daily diet. The German issue of 1,500 calories daily was simply inadequate. The German daily issue of hot water was for tea or ersatz coffee, which was also the German issue. The jam, margarine, and tea were all ersatz and had a horrible taste. Soup was a watery mixture of vegetables, cabbage, or kohlrabi, with a piece of meat the size of your finger in every five gallons. Some weeks, there were no food parcels. The black bread issued by the Germans reputedly contained sawdust and had the consistency of heavy muck and a sour taste, and it could be sliced about an eighth of an inch in thickness. A loaf weighed about five pounds, and the ration was approximately one loaf per man per week. Toasting helped overcome the sour taste and soggy texture.

As the war wound down and transportation became a severe problem, we received fewer and fewer Red Cross parcels. Instead of each man receiving his own parcel each week, he now had to share it with others, if indeed the parcels got through at all. The contents of the parcels differed, depending on the country of origin, but typically they contained a wide variety of items.

To exist, hidden talents and latent skills were developed to provide the necessities of life. Materials from Red Cross parcels were converted into tools, such as hacksaws made from the steel bands that were wrapped around the cardboard cartons. Plywood packing crates were turned into cupboards and room furniture. Tin cans supplemented by barbed wire were converted into practical appliances, such as cracker grinders, stoves, and even ovens.

Necessity is the mother of invention, and many of the inventions the guys came up with were truly remarkable. For example, using the metal from a KLIM can, which contained powdered milk, they produced all kinds of imaginative things. We called this process "tin-genuity."

We often dreamed of escape, but we knew this was not a realistic possibility, although some men certainly tried. After all, most of us did not speak German, and certainly no one would have mistaken me for a German. We also knew about the Great Escape and the execution of the 50 prisoners who were caught. Yes, executing a prisoner for attempting an escape was a violation of the Geneva Convention, but that certainly did not help those killed by the SS. In my drawing, two prisoners have been caught red-handed by a "ferret," which is what we called the guards who sneaked around the compound, on constant patrol, looking for trouble. Many times, "ferrets" could be seen and heard under the barracks, prodding the sand with long probes, looking for tunnels. They could enter rooms unannounced, listen at windows, or search anyone they considered suspicious. The two *Kriegies* in the drawing were caught with wire cutters and a piece of the fence they had snipped. They spent 10 days in the cooler on bread and water for their transgressions. Most of the time, ferrets were shadowed by the security section of the *Kriegie* escape committee, which oversaw any escape attempts.

Sometimes, when we were out for morning *Appell* or just wandering around, a German FW 190 would buzz the camp, I suppose to impress us pilots with his flying skills.

My drawing of a small plane symbolizes the astonishment that we experienced when the Me 262 went exploding across the camp at treetop height. We had never seen nor heard of a jet plane, so it came as a brain-busting surprise to us propeller drivers. I did not depict the Me 262 in these drawings because of the fear that German guards would confiscate my drawings if I had done so. But I did renditions of the jet planes on small pieces of paper.

For someone in captivity, Saturday nights were always tough. There you sat, slumped over, wondering what the guys were doing back home and whether they were getting all the girls.

Sleeping was always a popular pastime for POWs, especially on Sunday morning, when we were sometimes allowed extra time in the sack. Sunday was the only day that we did not have to get up and stand *Appell* (roll call). The German sergeant would walk down the ranks and count off the number of *Kriegies* to make sure that

Kriegie *brew.*

Kriegie *dreams.*

The barracks stove.

Red Cross parcels.

Contents of Red Cross parcels.

TINGENUITY +

ADD TO THE INGENUITY OF THE KRIEGSEFANGENEN, A PILE OF EMPTY KLIM TINS AND THE ARTISTRY OF THE "TIN BASHER" — THE RESULT WILL SATISFY MANY NEEDS OF THE P.O.W.

OUR OWN DANNY HAS PROVIDED ROOM 8 WITH PANS — AN OVEN — SPUD PEELER — CLOTHS PRANGER — COFFEE POT — CARROT SLICER ETC.

A FEW EXAMPLES OF SOUTH CMPD. PRODUCTS; A CLOCK FACE, GERMAN DOLLAR WATCH WORKS WITHIN; AN ACCURATE ZINC-TIN THERMOMETER, WITH CENTIGRADE AND FARENHEIT SCALES; A BAROMETER; CRACKER-GRINDER; SAND FILLED FLAT-IRONS; TIN SUIT-CASES; BLOW TORCHES FOR SOLDERING (SOLDER EXTRACTED BIT BY BIT FROM TOP OF ROAST-BEEF CANS; TEA STRAINERS; PICTURE FRAMES; ET CETERA. PLUS KRIEGIE BURNERS — LITTLE GIANTS — BURN CARDBOARD — BEDBOARDS — PAPER-OPERATE ON GAS PRINCIPAL. BLOWERS ATTACHED — WHITE HOT HEAT

Tin-genius inventions

Vas ist los? *A ferret on the hunt.*

A buzz job from the Luftwaffe.

all were present. It was not unusual to stand for hours when the count was incorrect because a prisoner was asleep in his sack. These roll calls became a convenient time for the German guards to make their periodic searches of the barracks looking for escape activities.

Sleep, however, was often a mixed blessing. It was wonderful when you dreamed of all the good times you were planning to enjoy when you got back home, but more often, sleep resulted in nightmares about the horrors of combat, including casualties, captivity, and death.

The mental after-effects of the fast and deadly battles in the skies over Germany took its toll, often in one's dreams. Many of us saw fellow flyers killed by 20mm shells in the surrounding skies and have ourselves looked into the jaws of enemy fighters coming at us from six different directions: shells bursting everywhere, two or three engines out, props that cannot be feathered, fire out of control, plane out of control, hitting the silk, floating down, traveling to a POW camp, and the prolonged sitting and waiting for the war to be over. Not surprisingly, many boys of 18 soon looked like 28, and then turned into old men in the space of a few months.

Of course, there were also daytime nightmares when we wondered whether our sweethearts were remaining faithful. All kinds of fearsome images clouded our minds, especially about the lurid and eager creatures on the home front who might be courting our girlfriends.

You can imagine what the *Kriegie* thought of the draft dodger. The irony of the situation was that the draft dodger was the one who was taking the *Kriegie*'s place with his girlfriend. I have no idea who was the original author of "The Draft Dodger." I just kept a copy of it when it passed through our barracks.

Mail was all-important. I started writing letters home as soon as I was captured. My family eventually got all of them, but, unfortunately, I never got any of their letters. Until the end of October 1944, they feared I had been killed in action. Then there was some kind of mix-up in the mail, so my mail never did catch up with me.

For those who did receive letters, there was nothing crueler than receiving the proverbial "Dear John" letter. For such unfortunate prisoners, their world had come to a double end.

"Dear Lieutenant" letters were heartbreakers. They often informed the *Kriegie* that the girl who had sworn that she would remain true and that he was her "one and only" had married someone else but then added, "Come to see us; I know that you will like him." Many of these letters were placed on the bulletin boards so that *Kriegies* could stay up to date on how their girlfriends were being cared for back home.

We had access to a German-language newspaper called *Der Beobachter* (*The Observer*). Of course, most of us couldn't read the articles, unless someone translated them for us. The cartoons were much easier to understand, and I traced several of them by holding them up to the window.

The craziest thing about my five months in Stalag Luft III was that I was never really scared. Maybe I was too dumb to be scared, but somehow I psychologically understood that I was just going to have to sit out my captivity.

Like most of the POW camps, we had radios in Stalag Luft III. The guys either constructed them, as they did everything else, from materials taken from Red Cross parcels, or the radios had been smuggled into camp. These radios allowed us to keep up with the war news. The Germans also maintained a bulletin board on the cookhouse wall, which contained all kinds of informational items, such as forthcoming athletic contests and dramatic and musical presentations. The cookhouse was a long wooden building where the German rations of soup and other communal foods were prepared and then distributed. The vats in the kitchens were used mostly to supply hot water for coffee and other "brews" and for washing. Each room could obtain two jugs of hot water each day: one at noon and one in the afternoon. However, soup made of potatoes, barley, dried vegetables, and meat stock was cooked in the kitchens four times a week and issued at the noon meals. Ground meat was also occasionally issued. There was a loudspeaker on the cookhouse wall to the right of the clock for broadcasting daily news. News items were also posted on the wall. Of course, we had our own rumors, the most popular of which was the invasion was about to happen— maybe even next week! Finally, there was a map that showed the progress of the war. Its depiction of the front lines was always two or three days old, so our radios were more current.

With all the information we had at our disposal, we were very much aware that the Russians were pushing back the German army and that the war would soon be over, but we didn't know exactly when. We also realized that it would likely be the Russian army that liberated us, but because the Germans also knew this, on the very cold night of January 27, 1945, the camp officials forced us to evacuate Stalag Luft III.

Saturday night blues.
'Nuff said!

Stalag nightmare.

Daytime nightmares.

The Draft Dodger.

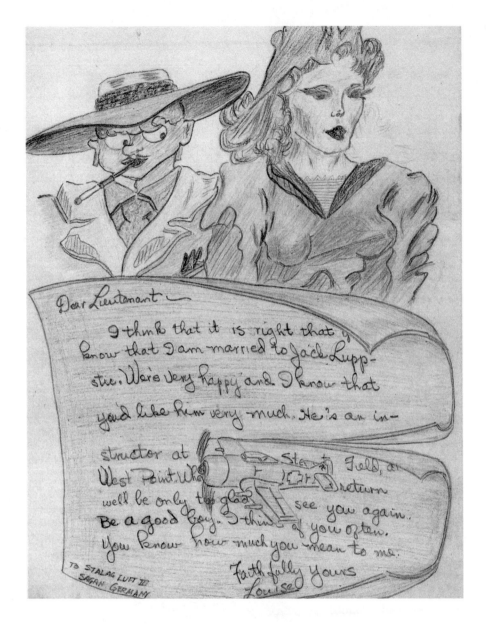

German cartoon:
"Roosevelt prays: 'Dear
God, bless our profits
that our brave boys have
not died in vain.'" Notice
Roosevelt's Semitic
advisers.

USA.- Luftganster morden europäische kinder

Die letze Lektion –

Zeichnung: Mjöinir

German cartoon: "USA: air gangsters murder European children." "Oh the humanity" is written on the blackboard; the lower caption reads, "The final lesson."

German cartoon: "Roosevelt's low-altitude war against women and children." Notice "Murder, Inc." written on the side of the American plane and Roosevelt's embracing of the Bible and the black pilot.

Nach der großen Abfuhr der Luftgangster

„Dammed – das mußte ja schief gehen! Nicht bei Nacht und Nebel Wolken und Sturm – –"

German cartoon: "After the final descent of the air gangsters: 'Damn, something must have gone wrong to keep us from our appointed rounds.'" For political and psychological reasons, the Germans referred to the American airmen as Luft-gangsters (air gangsters). Of course, we POWs glorified in this terminology.

The cookhouse wall.

7 Stalag VIIA and Liberation

When the Russian army started its final winter offensive through Poland and into Germany during the latter part of January, 1945, temperatures were at record lows, with lots of snow on the ground. We knew from our radios and the cookhouse map that the Russians had taken Warsaw and Kraków and were advancing toward us. Then, on the evening of January 27, 1945, while we were watching the play *You Can't Take It with You*, put on by our fellow prisoners in the camp theater, Colonel Goodrich came in and announced that we had 30 minutes to pack up and be ready to evacuate the camp.

The Luftwaffe officers in charge of our camp simply could not allow several thousand highly trained Allied airmen to be rescued by the advancing Russians, so we were ordered to fall out for a forced march. We were told to carry nothing with us except food and clothing. Word was passed down to take sustaining types of food, such as sugar, candy bars, and raisins rather than such items as powdered milk or potatoes. We rushed about getting our packs together in a kind of controlled pandemonium. We then put on as many items of clothing as we thought we could wear and still walk.

We did not know precisely where we were going, but we knew we were headed southwest toward the British and American lines and that the Russians were fast closing on us from the east. Spirits were high, but many of the men gorged themselves on food they had hoarded away and now could not take with them. Not surprisingly, they became sick, because their shrunken stomachs could not handle such large amounts of food, and this weakened them for the march.

Temperatures had dropped to 10 to 15 degrees below zero, and there were six to eight inches of newly fallen snow on the ground the night we left. Many of the men pulled their belongings on hastily improvised sleds, but when some of their buddies began to fall out, exhausted from the pace and their weakened physical condition, they allowed them to ride on their makeshift sleds, although they themselves were not in much better shape. Soon, exhausted men began throwing away letters, photographs, books, and all kinds of other personal items to lighten their loads.

I can still feel the bitter cold when my buddies from Room 8 and I started out walking at 11:00 that night. As far as the eye could see, there was a slow-moving column of men disappearing in the distance, and there were thousands more who would follow us out the gate later that night and the next morning. Our guards belonged to the *Volkssturm*, or People's Guard, made up of old men in their 60s and 70s who suffered much more than we did. In fact, it was not unusual for a *Kriegie* to help carry the rifle of one of these old guards who was having great difficulty keeping up. I saw several guards fall out from exhaustion, but no one seemed to pay much attention to them, and they probably froze to death. Fortunately for us, the Red Cross had recently provided us with new shoes, heavy socks, gloves, scarves, and overcoats.

We didn't dare stop to rest because we had to keep moving to keep warm. We walked all that first night, covering some 30 kilometers to Grosse Ställe, arriving at 10:00 the next morning. We rested in barns until late that afternoon. Although I was dead tired, I jotted down in my small notebook the names of the small towns we passed through and the mileage that showed up periodically on the road signs.

We started walking again that second evening, and this was the most excruciating part of the entire journey. The temperature was still bone-chilling, at least 10 degrees below zero, with a wind chill that made it feel even colder. Many of the guys will remember the long flat stretch of land where the cold wind hit us head on and seemed to go right through us. The only food we had was what we carried with us. Then the land became very hilly, and things really got rough. Clearly, we were too exhausted, hungry, and physically weakened to endure the demands of a forced march.

We arrived in Muskau at two in the morning of the 29th, after now having covered approximately 55 kilometers. We stayed in a large brick factory where we were able at least to dry our socks, fix our shoes and gloves, and get a little rest. It was warm and dry, and we were even able to wash. We also got our first German issue of black bread and margarine. Our rest was all too brief because the prisoners who had left Stalag Luft III after we did were pushing their way behind us.

After a rest of about eight hours, we left for the tiny village of Graustein, about 25 kilometers away, at 8:30 in the morning and arrived at 6:00 in the evening. We were assigned to a barn where we slept, crowded on top of each other for warmth. We left the next morning at 8:30 and arrived three hours later in Spremberg, which was a large town a few miles to the south. We were briefly housed in a brick building that someone said had been a Gestapo training school, before we left at 8:00 that evening by train for Moosburg and Stalag VIIA. In our exhausted condition, we were loaded on filthy and terribly crowded cattle cars for a two-day "ride" to Moosburg, which was located just northeast of Munich. These were the infamous "40 & 8" boxcars, which were supposed to have enough room for 40 men or eight horses, but we were packed in some 80 men to a car. The trip across Germany was excruciating. We were so crowded that some of us had to stand while others rested. We had no food, water, heat, or room to stretch our legs. When we did get a chance to sit down, we had to sit in the animal excrement of the previous occupants. Some boxcars had "indoor plumbing," which consisted of a small tin can that quickly overflowed. Some cars had no such can, so the armed guards permitted us to drop our pants and relieve ourselves when we stopped, generally at train stations in towns such as Chemnitz, Mosel, and Regensburg, and usually in full view of women and children. There we were, rows of POW "mooners"!

We arrived at Stalag VIIA at Moosburg on February 3, 1945. The place was a nightmare, with tens of thousands of men arriving from other prison camps. There was insufficient housing and very poor sanitary conditions. We were deloused, and initially assigned to large tents for two days that held 250 men each. We slept on the ground, which was covered with wood shavings, in our clothing, under blankets they gave us. We were then put in 180-foot barracks that held 225 men. The barracks were dingy, stucco-walled, and poorly lighted. We had the usual three-tiered, side-by-side, wooden-framed bunks, with a cotton sack filled with straw for a mattress. Everything was filthy and so infested with bedbugs, fleas, and other vermin that we decided to go back outside and sleep in the tents.

I drew only one sketch of the barracks in Stalag VIIA. As I look at this drawing today, I must say that it in no way captures the dreadful conditions we were forced to endure.

The Germans provided us with no cooking facilities, and the little food they gave us consisted of watery soup and black bread with slices of cheese, margarine, or blood sausage, but we did receive our first Red Cross food parcels since leaving Sagan. However, over the next few months, these parcels arrived infrequently, and when

*P-51 Red Tails strafing the train
station in Moosburg, Germany.*

they did, each man often received only a part of a parcel. We cooked our food on burners and blowers we made out of tin cans, Red Cross boxes, and wire. A small piece of wood the size of your hand provided enough heat to boil water for five men for tea or soup; and for fuel, we burned the bed boards, inner flooring of the barracks, and anything else we could scavenge.

We had pit toilets that quickly filled up and overflowed, sending their effluents out onto the ground and into our living areas. To make matters worse, the majority of us were suffering from diarrhea.

Stalag VIIA held approximately 100,000 Allied POWs, including some 45,000 Americans. Our immediate neighbors were turbaned Indians. Across the fence from us were Poles and Russians and other prisoners whom the Germans treated worse than cattle. However, we all suffered hunger pangs, a lack of heat, and even minimal medical care. The lice and fleas also did not discriminate.

One day, we heard the unmistakable roar of P-51s flying at treetop levels. Someone came running by and yelled, "Hey, Jeff, there are a bunch of Red Tailed P-51s in a square traffic pattern, taking turns shooting at something on the ground!" The entire camp ran out in the compound, yelling and jumping up and down, shouting and clapping our hands. The P-51s were in a luftberry, shooting up the Moosburg Train Station. These Red Tails were from the 332nd Fighter Group—my unit!

Our days were pretty much taken up with watching our planes fly overhead and waiting for our Red Cross parcels to arrive. We could hear the loud explosions when our heavies (heavy bombers) hit Munich, which was less than 20 miles southwest of us. This always made us feel good, but our emotions ran in the opposite direction when we witnessed one of our planes go down. We were also on an emotional roller coaster with our Red Cross food packages. I remember in late February being depressed because we supposedly had only enough food parcels to last a week. But then our spirits soared over a rumor that full parcels from Switzerland would soon be arriving, which might mean we would have one man to a parcel instead of two, three, or even four.

Rumors kept us going, especially as the front lines closed in on us. Each day, we heard reports on how close our troops were to Moosburg. Of course, we wondered whether the Germans would move us again, but on April 24, we were told we would not be moved, although General George Patton and his troops were supposedly only

Dawn Patrol!

40 kilometers away. Four days later, we knew we weren't going anywhere because the guards started to pack their belongings. The next morning there was no *Appell*. A guard told us about a Munich uprising and a huge tank battle only 10 kilometers away. By that time, we could also hear the guns and see flares.

April 29, 1945! Liberation! At 9:00 in the morning, the BBC reported Germany's unconditional surrender. At 10:00, a P-51 buzzed the camp at 100 feet. P-47s dive-bombed Moosburg only a mile away. We could hear gunfire just down the street from our main gate, and some of our guys were hit. At 11:45, several large American tanks and some line soldiers arrived at our main gate. German soldiers were at the other end of the camp, and a small skirmish erupted. A camp officer named Gladovich, who always treated us well and who after the war even attended some American POW reunions, ran out waving a white flag. At 12:42, the American flag was raised over the town of Moosburg. A few minutes later, we raised the American flag over the main gate of Stalag VIIA! One of the first things I did, after I knew the Germans were

Liberation Day in Stalag VIIA, April 29, 1945. Alexander Jefferson is standing in the lower-left corner, facing the camera. U.S. Army photo.

gone, was go to the camp headquarters building and take my German ID card out of the file (an image of that card is in Chapter 5). A lot of other guys did the same thing.

At precisely 1400 hours, or 2:00 in the afternoon, a Sherman tank from Patton's 14th Armored Division and an army jeep pulled into the camp. On May 1, Patton himself arrived, followed by several generals and colonels. The yelling and applause were thunderous. Some of us accompanied Patton on a tour of the camp. He entered one of the filthy barracks and asked whether it was for NCOs. When we told him, no, that these were officers' quarters, he nearly had a hemorrhage. No mattresses, and three blankets and one water pump for 300 men! He ordered food to be immediately brought in from Moosburg. A U.S. Army food kitchen arrived the next day and provided hot food for us by 4:00 in the afternoon. Cognac, wine, and champagne also mysteriously appeared. It was announced that in seven to nine days, we would be on our way to England, and shortly after that, we would be heading home. A payroll truck also rolled into camp, and all we had to do was sign our name and receive $80.00.

According to my notebook, on May 3, I hitched a ride in a Jeep and followed the American forces south to Dachau. I had heard there were a lot of dead bodies down the road, and I wanted to find out what that was all about. As we got closer to Dachau, I detected a nauseating odor, in the same way you can smell a barbecue on a warm summer day. Of course, this was the sickening smell of burned human flesh. The ovens were still warm when we entered Dachau.

The Dachau barracks were indescribable. There were thousands of striped-clothed skeletons lying on bunks or just milling around, and their sunken, hollow, vacant eyes still haunt me. Elsewhere, we found tables piled high with human hair and dental fixtures. There were corpses everywhere. Not surprisingly, I got violently ill.

A bulldozer gouged out a trench approximately 200 feet long by 20 feet wide. The former German guards were then forced to throw in the dead bodies, many of which were in various states of decay. Next, they spread lime over the corpses and covered them with dirt. I can tell you, whatever has been said or printed about Dachau, no one can fully or adequately describe what we found there.

We left Moosburg by truck at 8:00 in the morning of May 9 and drove to Landshut, about 50 kilometers to the northeast. From there, we flew to Verdunon on C-47s. After a two-week visit to Paris, about which I remember little except that the French women in Pigalle treated us like kings, we ended up on May 19 at Camp Lucky Strike, not far from the harbor at Le Havre. We were deloused, showered, given a typhus shot and a mock 64 (physical exam), processed, and assigned to tents in Area 23 where we got plenty of fine chow, including hard-boiled eggs, jam, and coffee.

On May 21, we went by truck to Le Havre and boarded the *USS Lejeune*, which was a navy transport. As a second lieutenant, I got the usual shaft and had to bunk down in the hole. We landed at Southampton, England, on May 23 and took on board some nurses and hospital cases. The next day, we left for the States in a convoy of four troop ships, five destroyers, one flat top, and 10 to 15 Liberty ships.

We steamed into New York on June 7. The ship's horns were blasting, and all of us were shouting at the top of our lungs. Spirits soared when the skyline of New York came into focus, and rose even higher when we spotted the Statue of Liberty and finally docked. What a feeling of indescribable jubilation! But then, going down the gangplank, a short, smug, white buck private shouted, "Whites to the right, niggers to the left."

It was very discouraging, upon returning to the United States, to find racism, segregation, and other social ills alive and well. I knew then I was back home.

8 Civilian!

Tuskegee instrument instructors, 1945.

After a stay of two days at Fort Dix, New Jersey, and a leave of 10 days followed by processing and reassignment in Atlantic City, I was assigned on August 25, 1945, to the Tuskegee Army Airfield as an instrument instructor in advanced training. A few months later, I was given additional duties as a flying instructor. I was making the princely sum of $250 per month, and life at postwar Tuskegee was absolute heaven. I loved flying during the day and partying most of the rest of the time.

Then one day I noticed a gorgeous bit of Alabama pulchritude flitting up and down the flight line. Her name was Adella Tucker McDonald, and she was a parachute rigger. When I first saw her, she was servicing parachutes for the various facilities at the airfield. Her co-worker was Winifred Davis, whose son, Major General Russell Davis, retired as commander of the Air National Guard. Well, one thing led to another, and Adella and I were married on October 16, 1946.

Caterpillar Club members whose parachutes were packed
by Adella Tucker McDonald:

M. R. Paige	August 10, 1942
D. E. Daly	October 31, 1945
S. B. Penn	May 12, 1946
S. Trudman	May 12, 1946

Lt. Paige was forced to bail out when his P-40 caught fire. He landed safely. The chute used by Paige was the first that Ms. McDonald had ever packed for use in the air.

By this time, the military had closed the Tuskegee Army Airfield, and the 332nd and I had been transferred to Lockbourne Army Air Base in Columbus, Ohio. By 1947, the military had stepped up the reduction of its forces, and many of us were riffed from active duty. I was discharged on January 16, 1947, but I did go into the Air Force Reserve, from which I retired in 1969 with the rank of Lieutenant Colonel. During my last three years in the Reserves, I was Staff Operations and Training Officer of the 90th Air Force Recovery Squadron at Willow Run Airport, just west of Detroit.

When Adella and I moved to Detroit in 1947 to begin our lives as civilians, my immediate prospects were not very promising. I desperately needed a job to support my new wife, but every time I applied for a position, I was told I was overqualified. I was even turned down for a job washing test tubes at pharmaceutical giant Parke-Davis. I had no better luck at Semet-Solvay, which was a fuel processing facility. While waiting to be interviewed at Semet-Solvay, I struck up a conversation with a young

*Alexander Jefferson, Adella Tucker
McDonald, and her best friend,
Louise, at TAAF Officer's Club, 1945.*

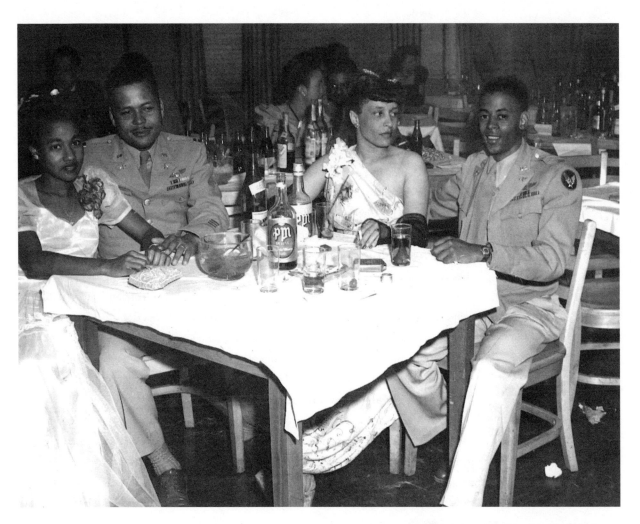

From left to right: Mrs. Woods, Carrol Woods, Adella Tucker McDonald, and Alexander Jefferson at TAAF Officer's Club, August 1945.

white boy who sat down next to me. I learned that he had just finished Chadsey High School, from where I had graduated 19 years earlier. When I was called in for my interview, I suggested we meet afterward and go out for a cup of coffee. Once again, I was told I was overqualified for the position. When the young man came out from his interview, he told me he had been offered the job that consisted of running the same kind of carbon analysis test on steel that I had performed five years earlier, after graduating from Clark.

I then decided to go back to school, believing that if I became even more qualified, a place in industry would surely open up. I made an appointment with the Wayne State University Chemistry Department, seeking admittance into its graduate program. I was told this would necessitate a year of remedial chemistry before I would even be ready to work on my master's degree. Naturally, I was very disappointed because I could not afford to take that much time.

As I was walking dejectedly across campus, I met an old friend, Leonard Sain, who was then teaching at Wayne State. He asked how I was doing, and when I told him, he suggested I talk to Dr. Billig, who was the supervisor for elementary school science education in the School of Education. Sain thought she would be able to help me because of my strong science background. With nothing to lose, and feeling the need to grasp at any straw, I rushed off to see her.

Dr. Billig looked at my record and said, "Mr. Jefferson, with your background in science, after a year of science education courses, I can assure you of a teaching position." This made sense to me, so I earned my teaching certificate at Wayne State and began teaching elementary science at Duffield Elementary School in the fall of 1948.

Adella Tucker McDonald Jefferson.

I have no regrets about my decision to enter the field of education because, for the most part, my career in the Detroit Public Schools was both enjoyable and rewarding.

I took classes during the day and worked for the U.S. Special Delivery Mail Service from 4:00 p.m. until 10:00 p.m. Monday through Friday and 10 hours on Saturday. I delivered all kinds of things, but I especially remember something called "State Sample dunners." State Sample was a furniture store on the corner of Michigan and State in downtown Detroit. These "dunners," which looked like a legal summons, warned that the recipient's wages were going to be garnished if payment for furniture was not forthcoming. This job got me through Wayne State University and put food on the table. I even kept it for a while after I began teaching.

I drove the area that would become zip code 48207. It covered roughly East Warren Avenue to the Detroit River and Woodward Avenue to East Grand Boulevard. This was Black Bottom, and white drivers refused to drive through it after dark, but for me it was like manna from heaven. I can still see myself, eleven o'clock at night, banging on the side of a rickety house with a flashlight, hollering, "Special delivery! Special delivery!" A door would cautiously open, and a voice would call out, "Who you want?" I would say, "Special delivery for so and so." The door would then swing open, the light and warmth of the room would engulf me, and the person would say, "Mailman, come on in and have a piece of chicken. How 'bout a beer?"

Adella and I had moved in with my parents on 28th Street, with the understanding that I would renovate the upstairs three rooms and stay there until we could accumulate enough money to buy our own home. It took me three months to put in new plasterboard walls, electrical circuits, windows, doors, toilet, shower, hot water tank, and an oil stove.

We didn't have two nickels to rub together, but Cohen and Melissa White, Bill and Julia Thomas, Maurice and Marge Letman, Mattie and Dennis Randolph, and all our kids would get together, and we did have fun. We would carry pillows to sit on, and blankets for our kids, because nobody had furniture. We were all in our late 20s, and we had some wild parties.

I taught during the day and drove special delivery at night, and Adella worked in an apron factory on 12th Street, four or five blocks south of Warren Avenue. We saved our money, and by the time our daughter Alexis Louise was born on June 7, 1949, we had accumulated more than $5,000. Now we needed a home more than ever, but there were a couple of problems: We discovered that it was almost impossible to get a mortgage, and there were few places in metropolitan Detroit where blacks could build a new house or even find one to buy. At that time, building a home in Southfield or Birmingham was a death wish for a black family. On the west side of Detroit, no black lived south of Warren Avenue, north of Tireman, or east of Epworth. Blacks also did not live north of Belmont or Trowbridge, and very few lived west of Woodward Avenue. Blacks were pretty much restricted to a corridor east of Woodward and south of Gratiot out to East Grand Boulevard.

The Jefferson home in Grixdale Park.

No white contractor was willing to consider us, even though we had our $5,000 down payment, until I found a German contractor by the name of Theodore L. DeGenhardt, who had begun building houses for blacks in the Conant Garden area. During the war, when the government built the nearby Sojourner Truth Project, whites had rioted to stop blacks from moving in, but now things were slowly beginning to open up. Conant Gardens consisted of about 30 square blocks isolated in northeastern Detroit, just south of 7 Mile Road and bordered on the east by Conant Street, the south by Nevada Street, and the west by Ryan Road.

Just to the west of Conant Gardens, the small neighborhood of Grixdale Park was also opening up, and we were able to purchase two lots for $1,800. At the time, whites still inhabited this neighborhood of small, aluminum siding homes, interspersed with many vacant lots, but they began moving out when blacks moved in. We hired DeGenhardt to build our home and were then able to secure an FHA mortgage for $8,200 through the United Savings Bank of Detroit. We moved into our new home on June 15, 1951.

Along with Harry and Viola Arnold, Leonard and Mae Godbee, and Edsel and Betty Stallings, we organized the Grixdale Park Property Owners Association. We were all young, energetic, and eager to beautify our new homes. I served as president for the first three years. Over the years, I also served in many other positions, and, to this day, I remain the association's agent, which the state of Michigan requires for all 501(c)(3) nonprofit organizations.

In 1951, we joined Rev. N. H. Holloway's Mitchell Memorial Methodist Church, today known as the Conant Avenue United Methodist Church. Over these past 50-some years, I have served my church on local, state, and national levels. I have been dean of an interracial camp at Judson Collins Camp and a delegate to the unification of the Methodist Church and the Evangelical United Brethren, which became the United Methodist Church in 1968. I served 10 years as youth counselor, seven years as youth choir director, and also as senior choir director, auditor, lay leader, trustee, and historian.

If you were a black teacher in Detroit in 1948, you taught at Duffield, Bishop, Miller, or Sampson. However, as the black population exploded, so too did the teaching assignments. I went to Pattengill Elementary School in 1954 and taught science there until 1969. The principal was Mary Alexander, who ruled the school with an iron fist. She had the distinction of being called "one of the seven devils," because she was one of seven white female principals who served as virtual dictators at their respective schools. She yelled at one and all, even the mailman if he didn't wipe his feet.

I received my master's degree in education in 1954 and then completed 30 hours past the master's in 1960. I was promoted to assistant principal in 1969, although at the time I opposed this assignment. I had passed the written exam four times for assistant principal, each time with a mark of better than 95 percent, but when it came time for the oral interview, I received only 40 percent. I was never given a reason why I failed these oral interviews, but I assumed it was because I appeared too aggressive and confrontational. Then, in 1970, central administration needed an African American administrator to quiet down a militant black school where the parents were dissatisfied with the white administration. I resisted transfer to Hally Elementary School for three weeks, until the administration convinced me that this was a real promotion and that my salary would increase by $3,000.

At the end of my first year at Halley, the principal, Gabriel Venticinque, was transferred to a small elementary school on the far west side, and Bernard Dent, who was black, became the new principal. This meant I had to leave because of an ironic new ruling that now required an integrated staff. I ended up at Ferry Elementary School, from which I retired as assistant principal in 1979.

One of my proudest postwar accomplishments was helping establish the Detroit chapter and later the national organization of Tuskegee Airmen. Ario Dixione, Richard Macon, Henry Peoples, Charley Hill, Wardell Polk, and some other Tuskegee Airmen had proposed an organizational meeting in Detroit. The question was where to hold it. My wife had died in 1970, so they said to me, "Jeff, you're single, how about having the meeting at your place?" On July 12, 1972, we held the first organizational meeting of the Detroit Chapter of the Tuskegee Airmen in my home. That same year we organized and hosted our first convention at the Tuller Hotel in downtown Detroit.

The Detroit chapter proved so successful that we helped organize similar chapters in Washington, DC and Philadelphia. The Tuskegee Airmen became incorporated in 1975, and we have more than 30 chapters, including chapters in Japan, Korea, Germany, England, and Alaska. We have several chapters on Air Force bases for young,

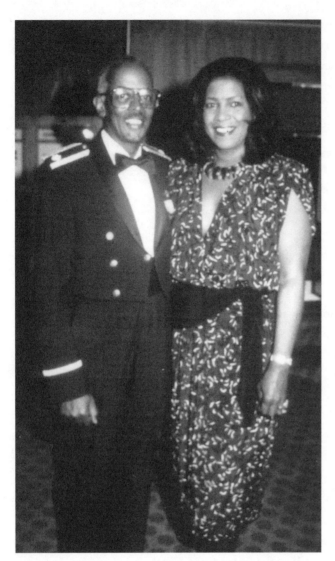

Alexander Jefferson and Lillian Eustace.

active duty personnel. Anyone may join, including civilians, because our objective is "to inspire young people in their educational and professional goals and to succeed in the fields of aviation and aerospace." We want others to learn our history and to spread our heritage. The officers and directors of the organization take no salaries or fees.

We preach education and ambition, especially to minority young people. We want them to become aware of the world of space technology and what it takes to live in it. Each year our National Scholarship Fund, which now totals more than $1,700,000, awards at least 40 $1,500 grants to deserving disadvantaged high school students. Applicants must have at least a three-point grade average on a four-point scale and be dedicated to a career in aviation, aeronautics, or aerospace. We tell them, "If you would like to go to a college or university or to the Air Force Academy, we'll provide counseling and guidance." In short, we want to do everything we can to help and inspire young people to become productive and fulfilled adults.

I was elected president of the Detroit chapter of the Tuskegee Airmen in 1974 and served as convention host president the following year, when we brought General Daniel "Chappie" James, Jr. in by helicopter onto the roof of Coho Hall. We had six black generals in attendance, but we couldn't get a single mainstream Detroit newspaper to give us coverage. I wonder why.

Over the years, I have also been active in the Tuskegee Airmen Speakers Bureau, which is headquartered in the Tuskegee Airmen National Historical Museum in Detroit's historic Fort Wayne. I speak to schools, churches, youth and senior groups,

From left to right: Tuskegee Airmen Alexander Jefferson, Robert Daniels, Richard Macon, and Bob Oneal were all shot down by ground fire in the south of France on August 12, 1944. Of the four, only Oneal, who was picked up by the French, escaped becoming a POW. This photo was taken at a Detroit reunion in 1972.

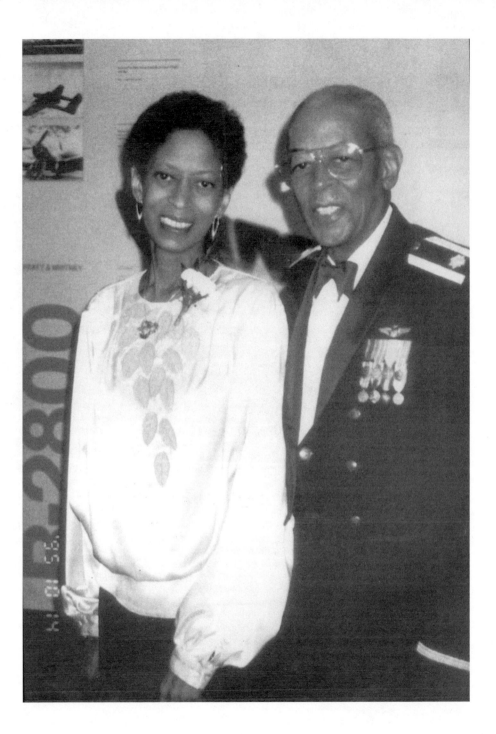

Alexander Jefferson and his daughter, Alexis, 1995.

military organizations, and a wide variety of other audiences. Over the past several years, I have averaged a speech per week.

I am a Life Member of the Silver Falcon Association of the U.S. Air Force Academy and have served since 1978, on a voluntary basis, as an admissions counselor for the Air Force Academy and the Air Force Reserve Officers Training Corps. I am also a Life Member of the American Ex-Prisoners of War and a Perpetual Member of the Military Order of the World Wars. Before she passed away, my wife and I had unofficially adopted a teenager, Ramon Robinson. He eventually became my son. Ramon was once in a swimming pool with a bunch of girls, and he said to one, "My pop should meet your mom." And so, Ramon was responsible for my meeting Lillian Eustace, who became my "significant other." Lillian has not missed a Tuskegee Convention, a P-40 Reunion, the Annual Jazz Cruise, or the Annual Week in Palm Desert since the early 1980s. The first thing my family says when we get together is, "Where's Lillian?" And the first thing her family says is, "Where's Mr. J?" Life is beautiful!

On October 14, 1995, I had the great honor of being enshrined in the Michigan Aviation Hall of Fame at the Kalamazoo Aviation Museum in Kalamazoo, Michigan. The Hall was established in 1987 for the purpose of honoring and preserving the history of outstanding Michigan air and space pioneers. Among its members are Roger B. Chaffee, Henry Ford, Clarence "Kelly" Johnson, William Powell Lear, Charles A. Lindbergh, Jack R. Lousma, James A. McDivitt, and Brewster H. Shaw Jr. Some of these individuals made aviation their life's work, while others volunteered their time, talent, energies, and insights. All represent the history and spirit of flight, including some who dreamed of its possibilities, others who made it a practical reality, and some who have shown the way to a limitless universe. I was selected for serving this country in one of its finest combat units, The Tuskegee Red Tails, along with my more than 30 years of dedicated service to the Michigan school system.

Lt. Col. Alexander Jefferson enshrined in the Michigan Aviation Hall of Fame, October 14, 1995.

■ U.S. Senator Debbie Stabenow also presented the
Bronze Star Medal to Lt.
Col. Alexander Jefferson for
his heroic service and meritorious achievements as a
Tuskegee Airman and POW
during World War II.

"Alexander Jefferson's story
is so inspiring and needs to be
told," said Stabenow. "As one
of the largest gatherings of its
kind in the world, presenting
this prestigious medal at the
Freedom Fund Dinner is a fit-
ting tribute."

Sen. Gary Peters (left), Lt. Col. Alexander Jefferson, Tuskegee
Airmen; Sen. Debbie Stabenow and Sen. Brenda Lawrence.

*Lt. Col. Alexander
Jefferson receiving
Bronze Star, May 2016.*

I was awarded the Purple Heart on November 9, 2001, authenticated by fellow POW Ewell
Ross McCright, who had been directed by the
senior American commander to interview every POW entering the South Compound. On
October 22, 2004, McCright was posthumously
awarded the Legion of Merit—the first American to earn the medal for service as a prisoner
of war.

It has been a busy life, and there's no sign
that it's slowing down. That's how it should be.
I'm happy to have been able to accomplish as much as I have during my lifetime,
and to have been a witness to so many positive changes, especially in the area of civil
rights. We Americans still face many challenges, but, in my mind, I remain convinced
that this is the finest country in the world.

On November 12, 2016, during the Tuskegee Airman National Historical Museum
28th Annual Salute Reception/Dinner, I was presented with the Knight of the Legion
of Honor medal by the French Consulate General, Pascale Furlong.

Postscript

The Tuskegee Airmen were dedicated, determined young men who volunteered to become America's first black military airmen. As pioneers, we were determined to serve the United States of America proudly and to the best of our ability, even though many of our fellow citizens, fellow aviators, and commanding officers believed that African Americans lacked intelligence, skill, courage, and patriotism.

On the training fields at Tuskegee, we were motivated to excel in everything we did, and that "push to excellence" is as valid today as it was when we were trying to prove to a doubting country that our commitment, skills, and determination matched, and often exceeded, those attributes in our white counterparts in the military. We were, of course, very different individually, but we had in common our sense of discipline, dignity, and accomplishment.

The Tuskegee Airmen, including the 10 civilian and military men and women who provided support for each of us pilots, as well as the other one million African Americans who served in World War II, all returned home determined to fight for civil rights for all Americans. We had fought with honor in the skies above and the battlefields below, but we still returned as segregated citizens, forced to continue our battles against bigotry and racism on the home front. White America was quite prepared to ignore the fact that the Tuskegee Airmen had earned 150 Distinguished Flying Crosses, one Legion of Merit, one Silver Star, two Soldier's Medals, 14 Bronze Stars, eight Purple Hearts, 95 Distinguished Flying Crosses, 744 Air Medals, and three Presidential Distinguished Unit Citations. Sixty-six of our men lost their lives in aerial combat, and even more were killed in training accidents. Another 32 of us became prisoners of war.

The Tuskegee Airmen would certainly have received many more prestigious medals if not for the color of our skin. The military's reluctance to award its highest commendations in World Wars I and II to African Americans is well known. After all, to have done so would have been an admission that past segregationist policies had been based on false assumptions. For example, no African American received the

Medal of Honor for his heroic actions in either World War I or II until 1997, when seven World War II black servicemen were belatedly so honored. Unfortunately, only one of them was then still alive to accept his medal.

As an African American, I had, of course, experienced discrimination throughout my life. Often it was covert, but it could also be overt. In graduate school, I had a history professor who literally called me a liar when I wrote a term paper on my experiences as a World War II fighter pilot. He told me that Negroes did not have the intelligence to enter the Air Force and that I had fabricated my story. He also did not believe a Negro could earn an "A" in his class because we supposedly were incapable of such high-quality work. I proved him wrong, but only after I went to the dean with my term paper along with the results of the tests I had taken in class.

The postwar civil rights movement was just beginning when I returned from service, but it profoundly affected my personal and professional life. It convinced me that so many things I had only dreamed of as a youth could now be part of my reality. As Tuskegee Airmen, we knew that we had served our country with distinction in battle, but now we also wanted to join the civil rights movement and do everything we could to break down the remaining racial barriers within both the military and civilian sectors.

Today discrimination tends to be more subtle, and it is often institutional. It is harder to discern when whites, usually male, get together in private clubs and businesses, in political and legal chambers, and even in institutions of higher learning to determine policies. Such decisions, of course, affect the well-being of all Americans, but especially African Americans, who historically have been absent from the seats of power. Nevertheless, our young people need to move beyond racism, just as we were forced to do when we were determined to fly. After all, if you are able to succeed in spite of the barriers erected by individuals and institutions, you emerge a much stronger human being.

Because we had clearly proven ourselves as airmen, we were confident that we could make the country we fought and died for a better place for all Americans. General Daniel "Chappie" James, Jr., who was one of the 992 Tuskegee pilots and who would later become the Air Force's first African American four-star general, said it best for all of us: "This is my country: I will hold her hand. I will fight for her. I shall protect her, but I'll make her treat me the way she should."

Dr. Alexander Jefferson

(Lt. Col. Ret.) U.S. Airforce

——Humanitarian——

Tuskegee Airman

Prisoner of War Survivor
Purple Heart Recipient
Biographical Author
2010 Rose Parade Float Rider

"God, Country, Pride then Self, Airmen Code"

Alexander Jefferson bio poster at Tournament of Roses Parade, 2010.

Tuskegee Airmen attend first convention sponsored by the Detroit chapter in Detroit, Michigan, in 1972. Front row, left to right: *unknown, Carr, Jefferson, Womack, Gen. Parrish, Gleed, Acher.* Second row: *unknown, Polk, Dixigné, Ragsdale, Browne, unknown, White.*

Christmas party, 1973. Detroit chapter at Maroogian Mansion basement with Coleman A. Young, DOTA/ Mayor of Detroit.

Alexander Jefferson was one of a hundred of the Tuskegee Airmen being honored at the Congressional Ceremony, March 2007.

Aging Tuskegee Airmen finally get a thank you

Black WWII fliers receive Congressional Gold Medal.

◆

By Ben Evans
ASSOCIATED PRESS

WASHINGTON — President Bush and Congress awarded the Tuskegee Airmen one of the nation's highest honors Thursday for fighting to defend their country even as they faced bigotry at home.

"Even the Nazis asked why African American men would fight for a country that treated them so unfairly," Bush told the group of legendary black aviators, who received a Congressional Gold Medal — the most prestigious Congress has to offer.

"For all the unreturned salutes and unforgivable indignities ... I salute you for your service to the United States of America," Bush told the airmen at the Capitol Rotunda ceremony as he stood in salute.

Some 300 of them — most well into their 80s — stood to return the gesture.

"We are so overjoyed," retired Capt. Roscoe Brown Jr. said, after he and five other airmen accepted the medal on behalf of the group. "We are so proud today, and I think America is proud today."

Nearly 1,000 fighter pilots trained as a segregated Army Air Corps unit at the Tuskegee, Ala., air base. President Franklin D. Roosevelt had overruled his top generals and ordered such a program be created.

Even after the black airmen were admitted, many commanders continued to believe they didn't have the intelligence, courage or patriotism to do what was being asked of them.

Not allowed to practice or fight with their white counterparts, the Tuskegee Airmen distinguished themselves by painting the tails of their airplanes red, which led to them becoming known as the "Red Tails."

Hundreds saw combat

DENNIS COOK/ASSOCIATED PRESS
President Bush salutes members of the Tuskegee Airmen during the Congressional Gold Medal ceremony in the Capitol Rotunda.

throughout Europe, the Mediterranean and North Africa, escorting bomber aircraft on missions and protecting them from the enemy.

Dozens died in the fighting; others were held prisoners of war.

"You caused America to look in the mirror of its soul, and you showed America that there was nothing a black person couldn't do," said Colin Powell, a retired Army general and Bush's former secretary of state.

Powell thanked the airmen for paving the way for his career.

Charles "A-Train" Dryden, 86, a retired lieutenant colonel from Atlanta, expressed mixed feelings that the honor came so long after the war and that many of his colleagues had died without knowing Americans appreciated their service.

Just a couple days ago, he said, a fellow pilot was hospital-

ized in Atlanta and couldn't attend the ceremony.

"So many of the guys have passed on," he said.

Dryden recalled his pride in returning from Africa and Europe after serving in Tuskegee's original 99th Fighter Squadron, only to be stationed in Walterboro, S.C., where he saw German prisoners of war get privileges in theaters and cafeterias denied to black soldiers.

"That was the low point of my career," Dryden said.

But Thursday's medal helped convince him the country now recognizes the airmen's contributions.

"It's really something," he said at a breakfast before the ceremony.

"It's never too late for your country to say that you've done a great job for us," retired Col. Elmer Jones, 89, of Arlington, Va., said this week.

President Bush saluting members of the Tuskegee Airmen during Congressional Medal ceremony.

Tuskegee Airmen were awarded the Congressional Gold Medal, March 29, 2007. Pictured from left to right: Charles McGhee, Lee Archer, Jefferson, Rosco Brown, and Pres. Bush.

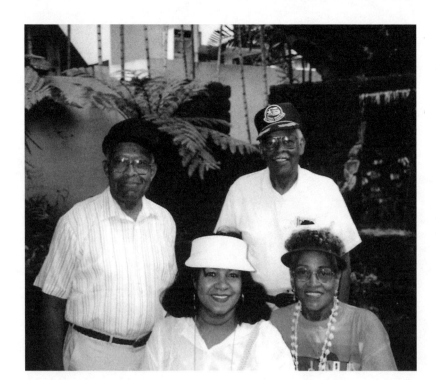

Jefferson (upper right) with sister, Emma Cobb (lower right), brother-in-law, Dumas, and Lillian Eustace.

Jefferson's ninetieth-birthday party (with family), 2011.

Jefferson's ninetieth-birthday party with his former fifth- and sixth-grade science students.

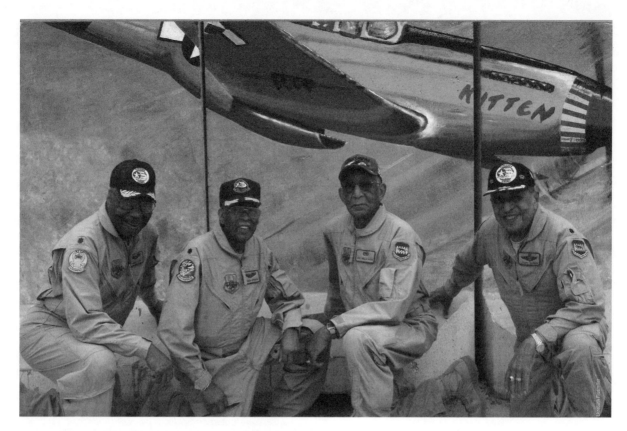

*Four of the original Tuskegee Airmen (*left to right: *Major George Boyd, Lt. Col. Alexander Jefferson, Staff Sgt. Philip Boome, and Lt. Col. James Warren) traveled to Balad, Iraq, to meet with Airmen of the 332nd AEW. The 332nd AEW traces its military lineage back to the Tuskegee Airmen (the 332nd Fighter Group).*

Alexander Jefferson and Tuskegee Airmen on Tournament of Roses Parade Float, 2010.

Gen. Benjamin O. Davis Jr. (second from left) admitted into Virginia Hall of Fame. Lt. Col. Alexander Jefferson (left), Col. Nate Carr, and Col. Leonard Isabelle Sr. attended the ceremony, 1993.

Fellow POW Captain Richard Macon and Alexander Jefferson at Thanksgiving Day parade in Detroit, Michigan, 1977.

Jefferson and General Colin Powell at a Tuskegee Airmen annual banquet.

Opportunity to meet and greet Air Force General Lester L. Lyles at a Tuskegee Airmen Convention.

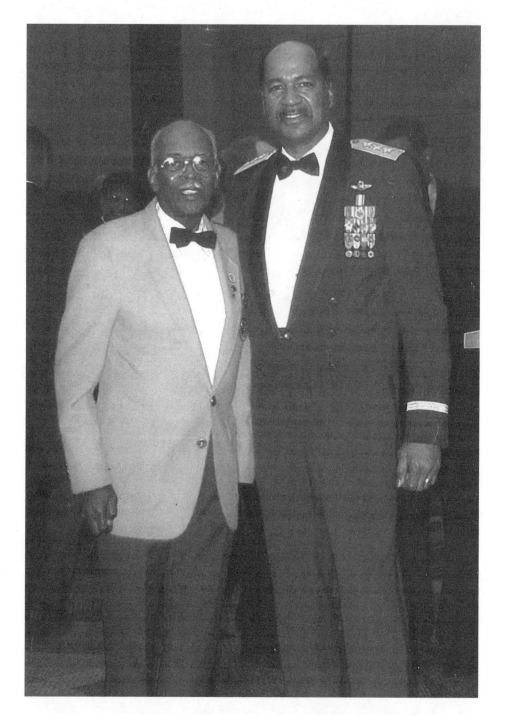

Opportunity to meet and greet Lt. General Daniel James III at a Tuskegee Airmen Convention, 2005.

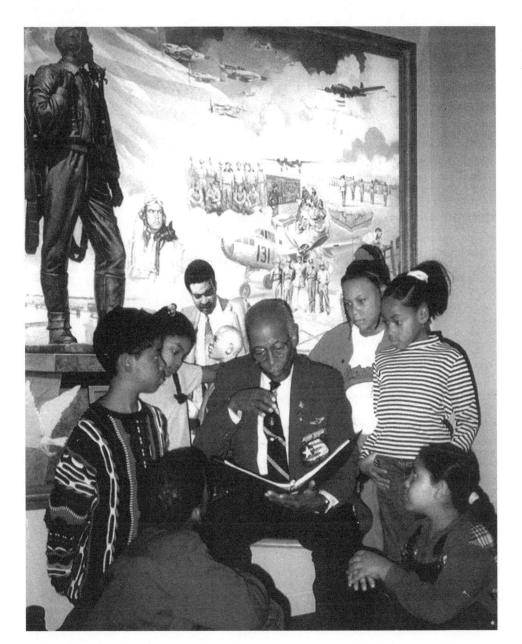

"The Legacy Continues":
Alexander Jefferson reading to
youth in the Tuskegee Airmen
Museum, Detroit, Michigan.

Coleman Young, the late mayor of Detroit and a Tuskegee Airman navigator in the 477th Bombardment Group, also emphasized our determination: "We learned how to survive in the air, and when we hit the ground, while white pilots rested, we continued our struggle to preserve our dignity as human beings. All of us are better and stronger for the experience."

Mayor Young was referring to the Double V campaign waged by all World War II African American servicemen and servicewomen. Simply put, we had to fight for victory on two fronts: first, against the racism of the Axis powers, and then against the segregation and discrimination of our own country.

Times have changed, and the social, economic, and, indeed, human compromises that we too often had been forced to make were no longer tenable in postwar America. Inclusion was the benchmark, and we took our first great postwar step on July 26, 1948, when President Harry S. Truman issued Executive Order 9981 calling for the desegregation of the Armed Forces. Without question, his decision was certainly made easier because of the wartime achievements of the Tuskegee Airmen. Next came the Supreme Court 1954 *Brown v. Board of Education* school desegregation decision, followed by the Civil Rights Acts of 1964, 1965, and 1968, all of which brought us closer to the ideal, expressed so well in 1776 by Thomas Jefferson and other signers of the Declaration of Independence that "all men are created equal [and] endowed by their creator with certain inalienable rights."

The social and legal changes of the postwar era also brought the Tuskegee Airmen the kind of official and popular recognition that they had long deserved. There are now more than 15 books about the Tuskegee Airmen, at least three documentaries, and one Hollywood feature film. We also have a special exhibit in the United State Air Force Museum at Wright-Patterson Air Force Base, just outside of Dayton, Ohio, as well as our own Tuskegee Airmen National Museum in Detroit.

Looking back, what did it all mean? Tuskegee Airman Ed Gleed said it so well for all of us: "When we were in training at Tuskegee and in combat, we never gave it a thought that we were making history. All we wanted was to learn to fly as Army Air Corps pilots, fight for our country, and survive."

Some 60 years have passed since we flew the unfriendly skies over Nazi Germany, but we Tuskegee Airmen are still fighter pilots. We have our reunions, and we reminisce and laugh about "the good old days." But we also are very proud of the changes that we helped bring about both within and outside the military. Above all, we want our fellow Americans to know that the civil rights we fought so hard for are not for African Americans alone, but for all human beings.

In the final analysis, the Tuskegee Airmen did make history, and I am so very proud to have been one of them.

Appendix

Alexander Jefferson's Organizational Affiliations

Air Force Association
American Ex-Prisoners of War Association of the
    United States
Clark-Atlanta University Alumni Association
Conant Avenue United Methodist Church: Chairman,
    Trustees, Committee
Detroit Organization of School Administrators
    and Supervisors
Ethnic Minority Higher Education Task Force,
    United Methodist Church
Howard University Alumni Association
Metropolitan Detroit Science Administrators
Michigan Association of Supervision and Curriculum
    Study
Michigan Retired Officers Association
Military Order of the World Wars
National Officers Association
P-40 Warhawk Pilot Association
P-51 Mustang Association
Reserve Officers Association of the United States
The Retired Officers Association
Tuskegee Airmen, Inc.
Wayne State University Alumni
Yankee Air Force

Alexander Jefferson's Military Awards

Air Force Achievement Medal
Air Force Longevity Service Medal
Air Medal
American Campaign Medal
American Defense Service Medal
Armed Forces Reserve Medal
Bronze Star Medal
European-African-Middle Eastern Campaign Medal
Knight of Legion of Honor Medal (France)
National Defense Service Medal
Prisoner of War Medal
Purple Heart
World War II Victory Medal

Selected Sources

Books

Beltrone, Art, and Lee Beltrone. *A Wartime Log*. Charlottesville, Va: Howell, 1995.

Bennett, Lerone. *Before the Mayflower: A History of Black America, 1619–1962*. Chicago: Johnson, 1969, 2000.

Bowers, William T., et al. *Black Soldier White Army*. Washington, DC: U.S. Government Printing Office, 1996.

Carlson, Lewis H. *We Were Each Other's Prisoners: An Oral History of World War II American and German Prisoners of War*. New York: Basic Books, 1997.

Dalfiume, Richard M. *Fighting on Two Fronts: Desegregation of the U.S. Armed Forces, 1939–1953*. Columbia: University of Missouri Press, 1969.

Daniel, Eugene L. *In the Presence of Mine Enemies: An American Chaplain in World War II German Prison Camps*. Attleboro, Mass: self-published, 1985.

Davis, Benjamin O., Jr. *Benjamin O. Davis, Jr., American: An Autobiography*. Washington, DC: Smithsonian Institution Press, 1991.

Davis, Lenwood G., and George Hill. *Blacks in the American Armed Forces, 1776–1983: A Bibliography*. Westport, Conn: Greenwood Press, 1985.

Dryden, Charles W. *A-Train: Memoirs of a Tuskegee Airman*. Tuscaloosa: University of Alabama Press, 1997.

Durand, Arthur. *Stalag Luft III: The Secret Story*. Baton Rouge: Louisiana State University Press, 1988.

Francis, Charles E., and Adolph Caso. *The Tuskegee Airmen: The Men Who Changed a Nation*. Boston: Branden, 1997.

———. *Tuskegee Airmen: The Story of the Negro in the U.S. Air Force*. Boston: Branden, 1993.

Franklin, John Hope. *From Slavery to Freedom: A History of Negro Americans*. New York: Knopf, 1947; repr. 1997.

George, Linda, and George Charles. *The Tuskegee Airmen*. Portsmouth, N.H.: Arcadia Tempus, 1998.

Greene, Robert Ewell. *A Pictorial Tribute to the Tuskegee Airmen*. Self-published, n.d.

Gropman, Alan L. *The Air Force Integrates, 1945–1964*. Washington, DC: U.S. Government Printing Office, 1978.

Gupert, Betty Kaplan. *Invisible Wings: An Annotated Bibliography on Blacks in Aviation, 1916–1993*. Westport, Conn: Greenwood Press, 1994.

Hardesty, Von, and Dominick Pisano. *Black Wings: The American Black in Aviation*. Washington, DC: Smithsonian Institution Press, 1984.

Homan, Lynn M., and Thomas Reilly. *Black Knights: The Story of the Tuskegee Airmen*. Gretna, La: Pelican, 2001.

Homan, Lynn M., et al. *Tuskegee Airmen: American Heroes*. Gretna, La: Pelican, 2002.

Jakeman, Robert J. *The Divided Skies: The Establishing Segregated Flight Training at Tuskegee, Alabama, 1934–1942*. Tuscaloosa: University of Alabama Press, 1992.

Kimball, R. W. *Clipped Wings*. Dayton, OH: R. W. Kimball, 1948; repr., Baltimore: Gateway, 1992.

King, Desmond. *Separate and Unequal: Black Americans and the U.S. Federal Government*. New York: Oxford University Press, 1997.

Lanning, Michael Lee. *The African-American Soldier: From Crispus Attucks to Colin Powell*. Secaucus, N.J.: Birch Lane Press, 1997.

Lee, Ulysses. *The Employment of the Negro Troops*. Washington, DC: U.S. Government Printing Office, 1966.

MacGregor, Morris J. *Integration of the Armed Forces, 1940–1965*. Washington, DC: U.S. Government Printing Office, 1981.

McGovern, James R. *Black Eagle: General Daniel "Chappie" James, Jr.* Tuscaloosa: University of Alabama Press, 1985.

McKee, Daniel C. *50 Years Later: Stalag Luft III Diary*. N. Richland Hills, Tex.: Smithfield Press, 1999.

McKissack, Patricia, et al. *Red-Tail Angels: The Story of the Tuskegee Airmen in World War II*. New York: Walker & Co., 2001.

Motley, Mary Penick, ed. *The Invisible Soldier: The Experiences of the Black Soldier, World War II*. Detroit: Wayne State University Press, 1975.

Neary, Bob. *Stalag Luft III: Sagan . . . Nuremberg . . . Moosburg: A Collection of German Prison Camp Sketches with Descriptive Text Based on Personal Experiences*. North Wales, Pa: self-published, 1946; repr., Eighth Air Force Association, 1992.

Nichols, Lee. *Breakthrough on the Color Front*. Pueblo, Colo: Passeggiata Press, 1993.

Osur, Alan M. *Blacks in the Army Air Forces During World War II: The Problem of Race Relations*. Washington, DC: U.S. Government Printing Office, 1977.

Phelps, J. Alfred. *Chappie: America's First Black Four-Star General: The Life and Times of Daniel James, Jr.* Novato, Calif: Presidio Press, 1991.

Rollins, Charles. *Stalag Luft III: The Full Story*. New York: Hyperion Books, 1992.

Rose, Robert A. *Lonely Eagles: The Story of America's Black Air Force in World War II*. Los Angeles: Tuskegee Airmen, Los Angeles Chapter, 1976.

Sandler, Stanley. *Segregated Skies: All-Black Combat Squadrons of WW II*. Washington, DC: Smithsonian Institution Press, 1992.

Scott, Lawrence P., and William M. Womack. *Double V: The Civil Rights Struggle of the Tuskegee Airmen*. East Lansing: Michigan State University Press, 1994.

Silvera, John D. *The Negro in World War II*. Manchester, N.H.: Ayer, 1974.

Smith, Charlene E. McGee, et al. *Tuskegee Airman: The Biography of Charles E. McGee, Air Force Fighter Combat Record Holder*. Boston: Branden, 1999.

Spivey, Delmar. *POW Odyssey: Recollections of Center Compound, Stalag Luft III and the Secret German Peace Mission in World War II*. Attleboro, Mass: Colonial Lithograph, 1984.

Takaki, Ronald T. *Double Victory: A Multicultural History of America in World War II*. Boston: Little, Brown, 2000.

Toliver, Raymond F. *The Interrogator: The Story of Hanns Joachim Scharff, Master Interrogator of the Luftwaffe*. Atglen, Pa: Schiffer Military History, 1997.

Warren, James C. *The Tuskegee Airmen Mutiny at Freeman Field*. San Rafael, Calif: Conyers, 1998.

White, Walter. *A Rising Wind. A Report on the Negro Soldier in the European Theatre of War*. Westport, Conn: Greenwood, 1978.

———. *A Man Called White: The Autobiography of Walter White*. New York: Viking Press, 1948.

Wright, Arnold A. *Behind the Wire: Stalag Luft III, South Compound*. Benton, Ark.: self-published, 1993.

Wynne, Neil A. *The Afro-American and the Second World War*. New York: Holmes and Meier, 1975.

Young, Coleman. *Hard Stuff: The Autobiography of Coleman Young*. New York: Viking Press, 1994.

Articles

"Air Force Ethics Once a Black, White Matter." *The State News* (Lansing, Mich.), May 13, 1983.

Baird, Woody. "Tuskegee Airmen Underscore Point They're Americans." *Huntsville Times*, August 19, 2001.

Boettcher, Thomas D. "Smithsonian Saluting Black Pilots." *Christian Science Monitor*, n.d.

Brooks, T. "Tuskegee Airmen Make Black History Come Alive." *Michigan Chronicle*, January 23–29, 2001.

Buck, Sue. "Former Tuskegee Airman Shares His Story at Cloverdale." *Farmington Observer*, January 17, 2002.

Cummings, Marc A. "The Tuskegee Airmen: Greatness in Our Midst." *Michigan Chronicle*, February 6, 2001.

Cole, James L. "Dulag Luft Recalled and Revisited." *Aero-space Historian* XIX (June 1972).

Friedheim, Eric. "Welcome to Dulag Luft." *Air Force* XX–VIII (September 1945).

Gavrilovich, Peter. "Air Force Removes Racial Reprimand from Black Aviators' WWII Record." *Detroit Free Press*, August 26, 1995.

———. "Tuskegee Airmen Helped U.S. Make Giant Leap." *Detroit Free Press*, July 18, 1989.

"The Genesis and Growth of the National Organization of Tuskegee Airmen, Inc." *Molding a Black Legacy*. Tuskegee Airmen, Inc., 1989.

Goldstein, Richard. "Gen. Benjamin O. Davis Jr, 89, Dies; Dispelled Racial Myths as Leader of Pilots' Unit." *The New York Times*, July 7, 2002.

Gropman, Alan. "Why the Services Are Integrated." *Air Force Times*, February 26, 1996.

Hennessy, Tom. "Race Never Grounded Ex-Pilot." *Long Beach Press-Telegram*, April 10, 2001.

Jackson, Irvin L. "Colonel Urges NAACP Crowd to Remember." *Port Huron Times Herald*, October 28, 1995.

Jefferson, Alexander. "Life as a Black POW." *Tony Brown's Journal* (March 1983).

Jefferson, Alexander, and Barbara Hoover. "North or South, He Was Hardened to Racism." *Detroit News*, February 16, 1990.

Kwan, Joshua L. "Tuskegee Airman Inspires Kids to Soar on Their Dreams." *San Jose Mercury News*, December 13, 2001.

Mackay, Katurah. "The Redtail Angels." *National Parks Magazine* (January/February 1999).

McClellan, Theresa D. "Air Legends: First Black Fighter Pilots Give Students Firsthand History Lesson." *Grand Rapids Press*, March 26, 2002.

McCollum, Berkley. "America's Forgotten Eagles." *Aviation Quarterly* 7, no. 2 (1983).

Moore, Lynn. "High Fliers: Airmen Describe Aerial Feats at Rocketry Event." *Muskegon Chronicle*, April 26, 2003.

"More Charges Leveled Against Selfridge Field." *Michigan Chronicle*, February 26, 1944.

Mullen, Frank. "Black Pilots' Past and Future Keep Stress on Excellence." *Denver Post*, August 7, 1981.

Palmer, Ken. "WW II Pilot Offers Words of Hope." *Flint Journal*, May 4, 2001.

Percy, William Alexander. "Jim Crow and Uncle Sam: The Tuskegee Flying Units and the U.S. Army Air Forces in Europe During World War II." *Journal of Military History* (July 2003).

Perry, Mylinda. "Pilot Helps Experiment, Air Force Integrated." *State News*, May 16, 1983.

Plammer, Philip, ed., "Dulag Luft." *Aerospace Historian* XIX (June 1972).

Rosencrantz, Rene A. "WW II Pilot Brings History to Life." *Clio Register*, January 26, 2003.

Scharff, Hans Joachim. "Without Torture." *Argosy* (May 1950).

"Selfridge Field Rumor Denied by War Department." *Michigan Chronicle*, May 13, 1944.

Strebe, Amy Goodpaster. "Red-Tailed Angel." *Mountain View Voice*, December 21, 2001.

"Tuskegee Airman Proud to Serve." *The Tennessean*, August 19, 2001.

"Tuskegee Airmen: Removal of Reprimands Was Long Overdue." *Detroit Free Press*, August 29, 1995.

Williams, Teresa Taylor. "Famous Airmen Reach Heights." *Muskegon Chronicle*, May 9, 1988.

Dissertations and Theses

Bland, Edwin A., Jr. "German Methods for Interrogation of Captured Allied Aircrews." M.A. thesis, Air Command and Staff School of Air University, Maxwell Air Force Base, 1948.

Burbank, Lyman B. "A History of the American Air Force Prisoners of War in Center Compound, Stalag Luft III, Germany." M.A. thesis, University of Chicago, 1946.

Goldman, Ben. "German Treatment of American Prisoners of War in World War II." M.A. thesis, Wayne State University, 1949.

Hasselbring, Andrew S. "American Prisoners of War in the Third Reich." Ph.D. dissertation, Temple University, 1991.

Films

Nightfighters: The True Story of the 332nd Fighter Group—The Tuskegee Airmen. Xenon Studios, 1994.

The Luft Gangster: Memoirs of a Second Class Hero. A Mike Rott Film, Dynasty Media Network LLC, 2016.

The Negro Soldier. U.S. Army, 1944.

The Tuskegee Airmen. HBO, 1995.

The Tuskegee Airmen. Rubicon Productions, 2003.

The Tuskegee Airmen: American Heroes. Goldhill Home Media, 1998.

Museums

Tuskegee Airmen National Museum, 6325 West Jefferson Ave., Detroit, MI 48209.

United States Air Force Museum, Wright-Patterson Air Force Base, Dayton, OH 45433.

Internet Sites and Publications

"Afro-Americans and the Military, 1939 to 1945." www.lib.umich.edu/clark-library

Brandon, MSgt. Linda E. "Black Pilots Shattered Myth." http://avstop.com/history/tuskegeeairmen/blackpilotsshattermyths.htm

Conyers Publishing Company. "The Tuskegee Airman Mutiny." www.tuskegee.com

The History Place. "African-Americans in World War II." www.historyplace.com/unitedstates/aframerwar

Lowe, Merrie Schilter. "Letters of Reprimand Removed from Tuskegee Airmen's Records." http://www.indianamilitary.org/ATTERBURYAAF/Tuskegee%20Airmen/TuskeggeAirmen.htm

McRae, Bennie J. "Tuskegee Airmen: Lest We Forget." http://lestweforget.hamptonu.edu/page.cfm?uuid=9FEC34DF-BD35-EC52-06AC946C7292C6D8

"Meet Lt. Colonel Alexander Jefferson." www.quest.nasa.gov/people/bios/aero/jeffersona.html

"Timeline of Events for African Americans in Military Service." https://www.army.mil/africanamericans/timeline.html#1939

"Tuskegee Airman Shares Experiences." http://www.fortcarsonmountaineer.com/2014/05/tuskegee-airman-shares-experiences/

"Tuskegee Airmen, Inc." http://tuskegeeairmen.org/

"Tuskegee Airmen of World War II." http://www.history.com/topics/world-war-ii/tuskegee-airmen

Other Sources

Russell, Kim. *Tuskegee Love Letters: Letters written by James B. Knighten and His Wife: A One-Act Play*. 702 Entertainment and Productions, n.d.

Tuskegee Airmen Trading Card Collector Sets. Long Beach, Calif: Mint Cards, n.d.

Index

World War II The Global, Human, and Ethical Dimension

G. KURT PIEHLER, series editor

Lawrence Cane, David E. Cane, Judy Barrett Litoff, and David C. Smith, eds.,
   *Fighting Fascism in Europe: The World War II Letters of an American Veteran
   of the Spanish Civil War*

Angelo M. Spinelli and Lewis H. Carlson, *Life behind Barbed Wire: The Secret World
   War II Photographs of Prisoner of War Angelo M. Spinelli*

Don Whitehead and John B. Romeiser, *"Beachhead Don": Reporting the War from the
   European Theater, 1942–1945*

Scott H. Bennett, ed., *Army GI, Pacifist CO: The World War II Letters of Frank and
   Albert Dietrich*

Alexander Jefferson with Lewis H. Carlson, *Red Tail Captured, Red Tail Free:
   Memoirs of a Tuskegee Airman and POW*

Jonathan G. Utley, *Going to War with Japan, 1937–1941*

Grant K. Goodman, *America's Japan: The First Year, 1945–1946*

Patricia Kollander with John O'Sullivan, *"I Must Be a Part of This War": One Man's
   Fight against Hitler and Nazism*

Judy Barrett Litoff, *An American Heroine in the French Resistance: The Diary and
   Memoir of Virginia d'Albert-Lake*

Thomas R. Christofferson and Michael S. Christofferson, *France during World War
   II: From Defeat to Liberation*

Don Whitehead, *Combat Reporter: Don Whitehead's World War II Diary and Memoirs*,
   edited by John B. Romeiser

James M. Gavin, *The General and His Daughter: The Wartime Letters of General
   James M. Gavin to His Daughter Barbara*, edited by Barbara Gavin Fauntleroy
   et al.

Carol Adele Kelly, ed., *Voices of My Comrades: America's Reserve Officers Remember
   World War II*, Foreword by Senators Ted Stevens and Daniel K. Inouye

John J. Toffey IV, *Jack Toffey's War: A Son's Memoir*

Lt. General James V. Edmundson, *Letters to Lee: From Pearl Harbor to the War's
   Final Mission*, edited by Dr. Celia Edmundson

John K. Stutterheim, *The Diary of Prisoner 17326: A Boy's Life in a Japanese Labor Camp*, Foreword by Mark Parillo

G. Kurt Piehler and Sidney Pash, eds., *The United States and the Second World War: New Perspectives on Diplomacy, War, and the Home Front*

Susan E. Wiant, *Between the Bylines: A Father's Legacy*, Foreword by Walter Cronkite

Deborah S. Cornelius, *Hungary in World War II: Caught in the Cauldron*

Gilya Gerda Schmidt, *Süssen Is Now Free of Jews: World War II, The Holocaust, and Rural Judaism*

Emanuel Rota, *A Pact with Vichy: Angelo Tasca from Italian Socialism to French Collaboration*

Panteleymon Anastasakis, *The Church of Greece under Axis Occupation*

Louise DeSalvo, *Chasing Ghosts: A Memoir of a Father, Gone to War*

Alexander Jefferson with Lewis H. Carlson, *Red Tail Captured, Red Tail Free: Memoirs of a Tuskegee Airman and POW, Revised Edition*